On November 20, 1972, Queen Elizabeth and Prince Philip will celebrate their silver wedding anniversary amid the flourishes and excitement that have followed them all of their lives. Of their twenty-five years of marriage, Elizabeth has for twenty been Queen of one of the most important countries in the world. For the royal couple this has meant maintaining an exacting and strenuous double role. As private individuals, devoted to their children, they have had to contend with the inevitable strain on marriage and family that is the result of continuous publicity and a staggering calendar of state occasions and official duties. As representatives of the British Commonwealth they are committed to their official responsibilities and the welfare of their subjects.

Judith Campbell has drawn a portrait, both candid and revealing, that is a tribute to the success of Elizabeth and Philip in both roles. Through the years, in spite of the enormous pressures, both Queen and consort have exhibited a rare wit, intelligence, and insight that have endeared them to family, friends, and millions of subjects.

The author traces the early years of their childhoods—Elizabeth as eldest child of England's royal family, Philip as Prince of Greece—and takes you through the difficult war years prior to their engagement. The idyllic early years of their marriage, when, for a

ELIZABETH & PHILIP

A Royal Love Story

ELIZABETH & PHILIP

A Royal Love Story

Judith Campbell

HENRY REGNERY COMPANY · CHICAGO

942.085
C

Contents

List of illustrations

ELIZABETH AND PHILIP

The Queen and Prince Philip wearing the Order of the Thistle (*Syndication International*)
The Investiture of the Prince of Wales (*London Express Photos*)
A Garden Party (*Sport and General Press Agency*)
A visit to the silk mills (*Syndication International*)
At the Highland Games (*Camera Press*)
In the Shetland Isles (*Syndication International*)
An unscheduled stop for Prince Philip at Cardiff (*Syndication International*)
The Queen in the underground (*Syndication International*)
A hippy accosts the Queen (*Syndication International*)
Talking to lorry drivers (*London Express Photos*)

between pages 52 and 53

President Nixon lunches at the Palace (*Associated Press*)
A state visit to France (*Syndication International*)
Welcoming President Eisenhower to Balmoral (*Syndication International*)
With Emperor Haile Selassie in Ethiopia (*London Express Photos*)
A tricky flight of steps at the ancient palace of Gondar (*London Express Photos*)
Prince Edward with astronaut Frank Borman (*Syndication International*)
Prince Philip in Morocco (*London Express Photos*)
Prince Philip takes the Queen to visit his old school (*London Express Photos*)
Returning from Canada (*Syndication International*)
Before a state banquet in Brussels (*London Express Photos*)
State visit to Chile (*London Express Photos*)
By boat to an evening party in Norway (*Overseas Photo and Feature Agency*)
The Royal Family on a 'walkabout' in New Zealand (*Camera Press*)
Prince Philip visiting the Parthenon (*Overseas Photo and Feature Agency*)
Well-insulated against the cold (*London Express Photos*)

between pages 68 and 69

The Royal Family at Badminton (*Syndication International*)
Waiting for the bride (*London Express Photos*)
In the gardens at Windsor (*Camera Press*)
First day at school (*London Express Photos*)
After the family race at Ascot (*Overseas Photo and Feature Agency*)
The Queen with her racehorse Carrozza (*London Express Photos*)
Members of the Royal Family out riding (*Overseas Photo and Feature Agency*)
The Queen driving her own car (*London Express Photos*)
Prince Philip's private helicopter (*London Express Photos*)

LIST OF ILLUSTRATIONS

between pages 84 and 85

Acknowledgements

The extracts from the letters of King George VI are quoted from Sir John Wheeler-Bennett's book *King George VI* and are republished by the gracious permission of Her Majesty The Queen.

The author would like to express her appreciation to Miss Anne Hawkins and Mr. William Heseltine in the Press Office at Buckingham Palace for their great help over dates, names and spellings.

Royal teamwork

THE Queen and Prince Philip will have been married twenty-five years on 20 November 1972. Perhaps, given the choice, they would have liked to celebrate this anniversary just within the family, and with no more outside interest and publicity than most people expect at such a time. But for Elizabeth the Second by the Grace of God of the United Kingdom of Great Britain and Northern Ireland and of Her other realms and Territories Queen, Head of the Commonwealth, Defender of the Faith, and for His Royal Highness the Prince Philip, Baron Greenwich, Earl of Merioneth, Duke of Edinburgh, KG, KT, there is no choice. For them publicity is inescapable, and whether it is a family celebration, state occasion or the day-to-day events of their personal life, it is all of absorbing interest to many millions of people in Britain and in a large proportion of the world.

Nor is this really surprising considering that, constitutional status included, the Queen and Prince Philip, in their unique working partnership, are required to embody the continuing demand of a modern, largely monarchist-minded democracy for the traditional glamour and romance of days long gone; hold thoroughly up-to-date views on life in general, and combine sufficient exclusiveness to preserve the essence of magic surrounding the throne, with the down-to-earth 'common touch' that enables people of all sorts and conditions to look on the royal family as a kind of extraordinary extension of their own. This is a difficult mixture with which the Queen and Prince Philip cope successfully, to the satisfaction of the majority, and in addition to bringing up a delightful family in an age when the parents' lot is often not an easy one.

Maybe the Queen and Prince Philip manage it all so well because, despite their different roles in a public life that is, to say the least, exacting, they contribute to the overall essentials as a team, and thoroughly enjoy their happy companionship.

Most people might find it difficult to define the exact constitutional position of the British monarchy nowadays, and many never realize that the larger part of the Queen's official work is done as head of state. And as head of state she must see to it that every speech she makes, apart from the 'declaring open' variety, is in accordance with existing government policy; indeed the minister concerned is given an opportunity to comment on it. This is where one important facet of the royal partnership comes in.

Prince Philip is a Privy Counsellor and early in the Queen's reign was specifically asked by the Government if he would look at state papers. Unlike Queen Victoria's Consort, Albert, Philip declined as he preferred not to be inhibited by having this kind of access to confidential government information. The Duke, therefore, does not see the state papers which, carried in the famous red boxes, daily pursue the Queen wherever she may be, nor is he a party to the more confidential aspects of her work. But without responsibility to any government department, and bounded only by common sense, he is free to voice his own opinions and to make suggestions.

Like the Queen, Prince Philip takes exceptional pains over his 'homework'. His job, which he created and does independently in addition to helping the Queen, concerns some 382 different organizations, of which he has real knowledge, and about which he has to speak at one time or another. This means usually eighty or ninety speeches a year, which he writes as well as delivers. Some of them go unremarked, some hit the headlines, a few reduce confirmed republicans to near-hysteria, others cause trepidation in high places. Most of them contain a core of plain good sense and contribute in some way to the common good. If it were possible to convey in cold, sober print that many of the disputable remarks are made 'tongue in cheek', there might be less commotion about some of the utterances of someone whose words can be as stimulating as his personality. And maybe, just occasionally, less fun for the originator.

To freedom of expression the Duke adds the liberty to come, go, talk, listen, probe and see for himself in a way that is obviously denied to the Queen. And from meetings, informal, formal and casual, with people of every kind of background, ideology and race, he gathers and brings back a vast fund of impressions, suggestions and solid information that is all part of the job, and makes a marvellous contribution to the teamwork.

The royal diary of engagements for the year is formidable enough, but nothing compared with the vast number of projects that have to be refused. Prince Philip often accompanies the Queen, but the majority of their duties are separate; in this way, by working independently they can also add to the number of acceptances.

ROYAL TEAMWORK

On ceremonial occasions and when the Queen sets off on Commonwealth or state visits, the Duke goes too. The Queen, moreover, would find it impossible to imagine coping with those marathon programmes without her husband there, backing her up with his natural charm, getting tetchy when he considers that she is being overtaxed, finding even moments of protocol funny, helping her with the new informality that is not always easy, and occasionally 'blowing his top', not always with justification.

Nowadays the technological marvels of the age make the lot of all public figures harder, and this certainly applies to the royal family. Not many years ago the tools used by the press and newsreel boys were still sufficiently unsophisticated to miss, as often as they recorded, the unguarded moment in public, the split second when it becomes imperative to scratch one's nose. Now, added to the sheer physical stamina required and to the bearing and expression proper to the occasion, is the daunting knowledge that at any moment one is subject to the closest, clearest scrutiny, sometimes by millions of people looking in on television.

Not that seasoned campaigners like the Queen and Prince Philip would consciously think about that aspect all the time, and possibly the secret of success is to forget and produce the likeable 'human' touches. Princess Anne, for example, forgetting that the microphones were on, made a natural complaint to her mother, something about a 'bloody scarf' getting in her eyes – a remark that was distinctly audible to members of the Australian press; or that moment inside Caernarvon Castle during the Prince of Wales's investiture in 1969, when the strain of the political squabbles and the unpleasant threats of the previous weeks were reflected briefly in a close-up of the Queen's face. It was towards the end of the ceremony, and when the cameras zoomed in, her tense expression was clearly seen. But they also lingered to pinpoint how she laughed and relaxed visibly when Prince Philip, watchful as always, made one of the light-hearted comments he conjures up to ease her path.

There is another side to it. Television gives millions more people the opportunity to see and enjoy all the traditional pomp and magnificence of the great state ceremonies, the glamour of a royal arrival at a command performance or the appearance of one of the family at a big sporting event. The immediacy of this medium stimulates the present popular demand to know public figures as people. The more people see of the royal family performing their public duties, the more they want to know of them apart from the crown, the gorgeous trappings and the fine uniforms. Despite the

Palace's very reasonable compliance with what is considered 'legitimate interest', and the great success of the *Royal Family* film, there are still numberless people who would like, but find it very difficult, to imagine the Queen and Prince Philip sitting at home drinking a cup of tea.

It is an aspect that is comparatively new. To ninety per cent of Queen Victoria's subjects she was the Queen, the Great Empress, the epitome of Victorian respectability, but very few would have known anything of the adventurous flesh-and-blood woman who loved setting out, voluminous petticoats, trailing habit and all, to explore the unknown Scottish Highlands on the broad back of a Highland pony. King George V and Queen Mary were held in much affectionate respect, but the King was genuinely surprised by the warmth of the London crowds celebrating his Silver Jubilee – because he never expected the people to like him for himself. Even George VI, the Queen's father, better known and loved and much closer to the 'common man' than any previous sovereign, considered his private life almost exclusively his own affair, a very understandable point of view for anyone whose life is largely public property.

But times change, opinions alter and, to survive, even an institution as traditional and honoured as the monarchy has to change too, in some ways, and to some extent. This is something that the Queen and Prince Philip and their advisers understand very well, accept and work at, although it is not always easy to estimate how far to go or where to draw the line. And the real success of any life in the public eye does depend largely on the home, and the family, and the fun and relaxation behind the scenes.

Considering the life they lead and contrary to what a great many people think, the Queen and Prince Philip have always managed to spend a lot of time with their young children. They try to keep the school-holiday periods clear, the Duke does his best to arrange his frequent travels abroad in term time, and state visits, like the one to Turkey in 1971, often take place in late autumn. In the Middle Ages any royal progressions round Britain had to be undertaken in the summer because the roads were impassable at any other time, and to some extent the custom lingers. Nowadays royal visits go on all through the year and regardless of weather – which is just as well considering that rain is traditionally 'Queen's weather' – but summer is still the peak time, before the family go to Scotland in early August.

The bulk of the year is spent at Buckingham Palace, originally Buckingham House, which was bought by George III and rebuilt by the architect John

The pre-war years, childhood and youth

King George VI described his family as a firm. On 20 November the present heads of the firm celebrate their Silver Wedding

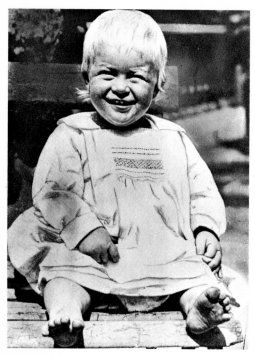

Philip was born in Corfu in 1921. This characteristically engaging photograph was taken when he was twelve months old

Philip at an Edinburgh sports meeting in 1935 when he was at school in Scotland

Princess Elizabeth and her sister enjoy a rare treat – Christmas shopping with their mother in 1938

The Queen's mother and father, King George and Queen Elizabeth, photographed by Baron on their Silver Wedding Anniversary

The Princesses
riding in Windsor
Great Park with
their father

A wartime family group in the Royal Lodge at Windsor in 1942

Princess Elizabeth and her sister at a children's fancy dress party

Elizabeth achieves her ambition to take an active part in warwork
like other girls of her age

ROYAL TEAMWORK

Nash in 1825. Prince Philip has called it both a museum and their 'tied cottage'. It has more than six hundred rooms, magnificent state apartments, the perfect settings for the ceremonies for which they were designed, and is filled with priceless works of art that, like the building, belong to the state. It is, furthermore, not the easiest of residences in which to create a home atmosphere. The corridors are of vast length – when the Queen lunches alone her tray is brought two hundred yards from the kitchens and then up two floors by lift. The stretch outside the schoolroom used to be used by Princess Anne pedalling a toy horse and cart, and has now been taken over by her youngest brother, Edward, as a place where he can practise soccer. The distance between the living apartments and the garden makes it imperative for the dogs to be removed for exercise at regular intervals.

The nursery wing, the rooms scarcely changed since the Queen was a child, is chiefly remarkable for its simplicity, and under the no-nonsense, affectionate care of Mabel Anderson, in charge since Anne was a little girl, there is a cheerful, easy air about it all that lacks typical nursery formality. Charles and Anne always breakfast in the nursery if they are at home, but the Prince of Wales, after five months with the RAF, is now serving a minimum of three years with the Navy, and is seldom there. And even when he was at university and in London for some of the vacations, he had reached an age when he was concerned with his own affairs for most of the time, and apart from when he dropped in to say good morning his parents did not see a great deal of him.

Princess Anne lives her own life, too. Often up, dressed in jeans and jodhpur boots, by seven o'clock, she drives herself, with her detective as passenger, down to Berkshire to school her Event horses before embarking on some public engagement. Some days she is in to lunch with the Queen, and Prince Philip if he is there, but otherwise in London they see little more of her than they did of Charles – and consider that this is how it should be. Both have encouraged their elder children to lead their own lives, although an independent full-time job for the Princess has so far proved elusive, and may prove an impossibility. The Queen and Prince Philip believe that as children grow up the parental role is chiefly to be there – when wanted. They are very conscious that it is not easy for their own family to adjust from the very different 'outside' world, where the young find most of their friends and amusements, to 'inside' where the homes and way of life can change only up to a certain point.

Basically, Buckingham Palace is the work centre of the regime, and right at the beginning there was a faint, but impracticable hope that it could be used entirely for the purpose, with Clarence House kept on as the home.

The Queen and Prince Philip have their offices close to each other on the first floor. Each day the Queen spends several hours at her desk reading through and signing state papers, dealing with an enormous volume of correspondence, some of which she answers personally, and in consultation with members of the five departments who help her run the monarchy and Palace. Afterwards she embarks on all the rest – perhaps one of the fourteen investitures, or some of the two to three hundred audiences she gives each year, the hairdressing and dressmakers' appointments, sittings for portraits, entertaining the annual influx of foreign guests, and some of the constant stream of public engagements that fill in most of what is left of each working day.

Prince Philip's office is the busiest in the entire Palace, the headquarters of his many-sided activities, and seat of the meticulous planning operations that often allow him to fit in several engagements, several hundreds of miles apart, in the same day.

All this explains something of why Buckingham Palace is the only one of the royal homes where the children, when young, have had to stick to a fairly rigid timetable for seeing their parents. But these times are set apart, and it has to be a very important engagement to interfere with the games downstairs after tea, the television watching, swimming with Prince Philip in the Palace pool, and the bedtime romps and reading that now concern only Edward.

One aspect of Buckingham Palace that contrasts with the imposing façade seen by the crowds of tourists peering through the gilt-topped railings outside is the pervading relaxed, friendly atmosphere inside. It starts with the pages, most of them unexpectedly middle-aged, whose amiable equanimity appears equal to anything – even to the caller who arrived in a blizzard, to slip up on the steps of the Privy Purse entrance in a welter of extraneous shopping-bags and a pair of rubber boots. The officers and staff of the Queen's Household, including those in the Press Office, who inhabit the ground-floor offices, usually with doors companionably ajar, are highly efficient, remarkably accessible, adamant when necessary, and always concerned to be helpful. There is also a light-hearted camaraderie abroad amongst them that is infectious, and not every conversation taking place between the various compartments via the intercom, the first of Prince Philip's modernizations, is as serious as might be thought. But then the level at which most associations operate is determined by those at the top.

ROYAL TEAMWORK

All the formality and glitter, the ceremonial, etiquette and protocol that make up the Court 'front', serve the purposes for which they exist – for instance all ambassadors are ensured of exactly similar treatment – but has nothing to do with the Court 'off duty'. King George VI, a first-class dancer, loved to lead the long snake of a conga up and down the staircases and along the corridors of the Palace. And nothing could be less stuffy or more fun than the family and household gatherings, their entertainments distinctly more hilarious than erudite, at such times as Christmas.

Even the assortment of conveyances coming and going at the Palace points to some of the extremes – the scarlet helicopter, piloted by Prince Philip, roaring up out of the grounds off the lawn; the Town Coach clattering in, drawn by a pair of royal carriage horses and bearing a new ambassador, come to present his credentials to the Queen; one of the four handsome maroon and black Rolls Royces, none now under ten years old, frequently used by the Queen on state and official occasions; one or other of the zippy cars owned respectively by Prince Philip, Prince Charles and Princess Anne and usually owner-driven. And once a year, in June, a horse, either one belonging to the mounted branch of the Metropolitan Police or Burmese, presented by the Royal Canadian Mounted Police, carries the Queen out under the central archway into a crescendo of cheering and crowd emotion that seems, in the first moment, an almost tangible barrier.

This is the occasion of the sovereign's Official Birthday Parade, the ceremony of Trooping the Colour that has taken place more or less regularly since 1805, and which the Queen, as Princess Elizabeth, first attended in an official capacity in 1947, when she rode beside the King.

Wearing the specially adapted, becoming uniform of a colonel-in-chief of the Foot Guards, usually attended by the Duke of Edinburgh, the Duke of Kent and other high-ranking officers and officials and escorted by the Household Cavalry, the Queen rides up the Mall to Horse Guards Parade, where her natural dignity and bearing set the tone for the ensuing splendid military spectacle, before she rides back to the Palace at the head of the Queen's Guard.

It is the only time the Queen rides side-saddle and, thorough as always, she practises for some weeks beforehand in the covered school at the Palace, riding with the person who helps re-accustom working police horses to this type of saddle and horsemanship. Occasionally Prince Philip appears, in order to familiarize his mount with the horse-scaring sight of a bearskin; the Queen Mother likes to meet any of her ex-steeplechasers now doing duty on the beat, and the police officers, who take a lot of pride in providing the Queen with her parade horse, bring along a selection of future candidates for the Queen to see and feed with carrots.

It is all very friendly, and as cheerful as the scenes just before and after the actual imposing ceremony. These are set in the Inner Quadrangle, where the horses are mounted, and later dismounted; from where the Queen Mother and some of her grandchildren drive off in an open barouche to the parade; where royal grooms flick at imagined specks on ceremonial bridles, and officers with magnificent titles – Gold-Stick-in-Waiting, Silver-Stick-in-Waiting and the rest – do wait with their horses, to fall in behind the Queen; where the Queen laughs and jokes with Prince Philip before and after riding out, appropriately decorous, on an annual occasion of traditional pageantry.

Elizabeth's childhood

ELIZABETH ALEXANDRA MARY, the Duke and Duchess of York's first child, was born on 21 April 1926 at 17 Bruton Street, the home of her maternal grandparents.

She arrived in a world where radio was still in its infancy and, although the inventor Baird had contrived by then to 'see' his office boy's face through an intervening wall, anything comparable to modern television must have seemed an unbelievable pipe-dream. It was a year when Stanley Baldwin was Prime Minister, London buses were still topless, airships were the 'in' thing and Coronach won the Derby. Adolf Hitler was then thirty-seven.

The soldiers who had returned from the war-to-end-all-wars had long ceased to believe in Lloyd George's Promised Land, but the idealistic hope of world peace, founded at Locarno the previous year, had not yet been shattered by worldwide economic depression. Even so, in Britain soaring unemployment, the dole, hunger, bitterness and eventually the closing of coalpits sparked off the beginning of a great social upheaval, the so-called General Strike, less than a month after Princess Elizabeth was born. Maybe the current top of the 1926 pops, 'I'm Sitting on Top of the World', rang true only for a minority, but it was a wonderfully exciting and vigorous decade in which to be born.

At the time of Elizabeth's birth her parents were living at White Lodge in Richmond Park, a royal residence, originally a 'simple place of refreshment after the chase' for George II, made available to them on their marriage four years previously. Within a year the house was proving too big, and while too far out of London for the Yorks' convenience, it was much too accessible for the sightseers who destroyed any privacy. A move, however, was not possible until 1927.

Before his marriage it is unlikely that the Duke of York would have been bothered by too much public interest. As a small boy, Elizabeth's father, named Albert to offset the impolitic accident of being born on the anniversary of the Prince Consort's death, was much more of an introvert than his forthcoming elder brother, the future Edward VIII. He was highly strung and affectionate, a bit of a dreamer, with an excitable temper and given to occasional moods of tearful depression, usually induced by the frustrations of the very bad stammer that was to plague him for so many years. Bertie, as they called him, tended to be eclipsed by Edward's easy, instinctive charm, and although both boys and their sister Mary were intelligent, high-spirited and as naughty as most children, their childhood was unlikely to make life easier for an ultra-sensitive boy with a distressing speech impediment.

Elizabeth was to remember their father, King George V, as a mellowed and devoted grandfather, but with his own youthful family he was very much the bluff, sometimes intolerant ex-naval officer, convinced he had 'a way' with children. This was true with children who were not his own, but a hasty manner combined with heavy-handed, misunderstood chaffing formed an unbridgeable gap between him and his own young sons.

The King had enjoyed a very happy childhood himself and he genuinely longed to recreate it for his own family. It was unfortunate that, again, some of the very qualities, such as a rigid sense of duty and a quarter-deck conception of discipline, that were to stand him in such good stead during the First World War, made him appear as a father unapproachable and something of a martinet. Both he and his wife, the lively minded Princess of Teck, who became Britain's much loved Queen Mary, were devoted to their children, but understandably she upheld her husband's views on parental discipline, and they both subscribed to the nursery-regimented Victorian methods of bringing up a family.

The children, all close together in age, contrived plenty of amusements among themselves and there were many good times together as a family, but even as a young man Prince Albert still seemed to be seeking the understanding and sensitive appreciation in his home life that he had lacked as a child.

Those who knew the Duke of York, as he was created in 1920, liked and respected his sincere, unassuming character. He was a first-class sportsman, and once over his initial shyness could be the best and gayest of companions. But the stammer was no better, and the Duke, quiet and reserved by nature, remained overshadowed by the magnetic personality of the then Prince of Wales; without the wide contacts allied to the position of Heir Apparent, he was relatively unknown to the public. This state of affairs continued until he made a marriage that appealed to people all over Britain, and found a companion who offset her husband's diffidence with her own spontaneous friendliness, and boosted his morale with the loving encouragement needed to bring out his many latent qualities.

Princess Elizabeth's mother, formerly Lady Elizabeth Bowes-Lyon, is the second youngest of the Earl of Strathmore's ten children. It was an exceptionally happy family, with the children on affectionate, unconstrained terms with their parents, a relationship that continued after they grew up. The gaiety and informality, the family jokes and freedom of expression that permeated the two Strathmore homes, were a revelation to the Duke of York when he first encountered them. Even before falling completely in love, he made up his mind that when he had children of his own this was the kind of atmosphere in which they should grow up, a decision to which he kept.

It took two years to persuade Lady Elizabeth to forsake the gay, free life of a young and pretty girl who had taken postwar London by storm for the considerably more confined and public life of a member of the royal family. Then at last, in January 1923, the Duke was able to announce his engagement, with the wholehearted approval of the King and Queen, and to the delight of the British and Empire public. The wedding took place three months later.

When their daughter Elizabeth was eight months old the King nominated her father to perform the opening ceremony of the Australian Parliament in Canberra, the new federal capital of the Dominion. It meant leaving Elizabeth for five months, but this is something often demanded of royal parents, and the Duke's pleasure and satisfaction at being proposed for such an important mission were marred only by his secret dread of all the speeches involved. Despite various treatments, his own courage and his wife's constant reassurance, the stammer remained. Then, only three months before they sailed, a new therapy was tried that resulted in an immediate improvement in the Duke's self-confidence and delivery. Eventually he was almost completely cured, although there would always be an occasional hesitancy, and the Duke never lost his dislike of public speaking, particularly of broadcasting.

That royal tour proved a great success on all counts, and by 1939 the Duke, then King, after delivering a fine speech on his return from Canada, was able to write, 'It was a change from the old days when speaking, I felt, was hell!' But long before then the ability to express himself clearly, in public and also at long last to his father, altered the Duke's entire outlook and contributed to the happiness of his family life. It may also have changed the course of history.

ELIZABETH AND PHILIP

No man was ever more reluctant to be king, both on his own account and on that of the daughter who would almost certainly succeed him. If the speech impediment had not been overcome before 1936 it is possible that the Duke, physically as well as emotionally unprepared, might have felt he could not take on such an overwhelming burden as the monarchy.

When she was born Elizabeth of York ranked third in the succession and it seemed unlikely she would ever accede to the throne. Her grandfather was still in good health, and although her Uncle Edward, the Heir Apparent, was still a bachelor, he was only thirty-two and it seemed unlikely that he would not eventually marry. Even if he had no children it was more than possible that the Duke of York would have a son, and any brothers would automatically take precedence over Elizabeth. But although her succession appeared remote, from the day she was born Elizabeth attracted a more than usual amount of interest, partly because of her parents' popularity and soon also on her own account.

The Yorks were determined that their daughter should not be spoiled by too much public adulation and that she should be able to enjoy a normal childhood as much as possible out of the public eye, but that was easier said than done. Even nowadays, when the approach to the royal family is much more down-to-earth and less sentimental, it has not been easy for the Queen and Prince Philip to keep their family in the background when young.

From the very first moment royal babies are *news*. A certain amount of legitimate publicity is inevitable and makes it impossible for them to lead lives exactly comparable to those of other children, and in some ways this is a good thing. Their lives always have to be restricted to some degree, and it must be much harder for those who marry into the regime after knowing the freedom and privacy most people can take for granted, than for those who grow up within the limits. This was a feeling that Prince Charles voiced when he said, '. . . The one advantage about marrying a princess for instance, or somebody from a royal family, is that they know what happens.' By the time she was nineteen the heart-free Princess Anne had discovered that it was easier for her to move in her friends' circles, than for those totally unacquainted with the conventions and restraints of royal life to move in hers.

When the Duke and Duchess of York returned from their Australasian tour they had three tons of presents with them, all sent for the baby back home. By then they had moved into London and were settled in the house, 145 Piccadilly, that was to be their town home for nearly ten years. Soon the only way to circumvent the crowds following the pram on the daily outings in Hyde Park, was to take to the landau and pair sometimes dispatched for the purpose from the Royal Mews by command of the King. Wherever Elizabeth appeared there were throngs of admirers to 'ooh' and 'aah' and exclaim over her. Although royal babies are taught to wave greetings at such an early age that they think it the normal thing to do, the time must come when they realize that other children neither receive nor give the same public welcome.

Elizabeth's sister, Margaret Rose, was born in 1930, and from then the load of adulation could at least be shared. Despite the four-year age gap, the sisters quickly became good friends, and grew up together sharing the fun and experience of a companionship made more than usually close by the circumstances of their life.

The nursery routine at 'No. 145' was much the same as that found in any well-to-do home of the period, but despite the Yorks' gay social life and numerous public duties there was never any question of wholly relegating the children's upbringing to nannies, however devoted. When Margaret was born, the Duchess engaged a new nursery-maid, Margaret Macdonald. This red-headed Scots girl, nicknamed Bobo, was to remain with her elder charge and in the years ahead became the Queen's official dresser, as well as her utterly discreet confidante and dedicated friend.

It was Elizabeth's good fortune to grow up in the security of a really loving home. If there is such a state as an ideal marriage then the Duke and Duchess of York achieved it. Each provided the perfect foil to the other's temperament, the Duchess's inherently happy outlook counterbalancing her husband's more volatile character, the serenity that is seldom disturbed helping her to calm his quick temper. They were so content in each other's company, so much the complement of one another that their children came to think and speak of their parents collectively rather than as two individuals. When it came to their daughters' upbringing the Duke and Duchess were always of one mind, and Elizabeth and Margaret were never able to 'play off' one parent against the other!

The Duke took the greatest interest in his daughters from the time they were tiny babies, and he and his wife were always most happy when they were all together as a family. Yet the children were not spoiled. Obedience, thought for others and good manners were insisted on, and faults were not overlooked. Since all children absorb some of the atmosphere in which they are brought up, it was fortunate for the future Queen that her father had inherited King George v's orderliness and liking for the customary progressions of royal life, and that, true to his naval training, the Duke was a stickler for punctuality, a virtue not always shared by his wife!

There was never any question as to how Elizabeth would be educated. Her younger uncles were sent to preparatory school, but her father and Uncle Edward were educated at home until each in turn, at the age of thirteen, entered the Royal Naval College, Osborne, as a cadet. Her aunt, Princess Mary, received home schooling as a matter of course, and her mother, like the majority of daughters of well-to-do families at that time, was educated by the family governess whose lessons were supplemented by the teachings of the gifted Countess of Strathmore.

Elizabeth followed suit, and her first lessons, including French, were given her by the Duchess. Since her mother had inherited Lady Strathmore's talents in music, art and dancing, she enjoyed instructing her own children in the same pleasant accomplishments.

A governess joined the household when Elizabeth was seven, and continued with her general education and Margaret's until the schoolroom was a thing of the past. The curriculum was expanded with the aid of occasional 'outside' teachers, but was never overburdened on the purely academic side. Both the Duke and Duchess disliked mathematics and had been unable to master the subject when they were young, and it never worried them that Elizabeth could not cope either. When she was thirteen, by then Heiress Presumptive for the past three years, the Provost of Eton was called in to start her on a course that would give her a thorough grounding in constitutional history, an essential subject for a potential sovereign.

Queen Mary, a devoted grandmother who had the greatest interest in her granddaughters, loved to take Elizabeth and Margaret to art galleries and exhibitions. Their governess also took them on unobtrusive outings round London to further their education, and to places of amusement such as the Zoo or 'Bekonscot', the model village at Beaconsfield. These little excursions, however discreet, usually produced another form of training, since the children seldom went unrecognized – a press photographer would materialize and people gather round, and it became yet another lesson in accepting publicity as a normal part of life.

Entertainments with the Duke and Duchess, usually such events as the International Horse Show or the Royal Tournament, inevitably became semi-official occasions. However far and free from the public gaze the annual holiday in Scotland might be in theory, there was always the Sunday drive to Crathie Church with the King and Queen, with the waving to enthusiastic visitors from the well-rugged depths of their grandparents' royal car or open carriage to re-emphasize their royal status.

Although the idea of Elizabeth's attending even a day school would never have been considered, her parents were anxious to avoid the disadvantages suffered by her father through the cloistered existence of his early years. There was the usual run of parties; the children took young friends to their own birthday entertainments and occasionally joined other families for theirs. After the accession a troop of Girl Guides, with a Brownie Pack for Margaret, was organized at the Palace, the members drawn from various walks of life. As they grew older, Elizabeth and Margaret were encouraged to produce and act in an annual Christmas pantomime, and this also involved an 'outside' cast.

During the later stages of the war, Elizabeth's contacts with the outside world increased, but even then her life, compared with that of her future daughter, was very sheltered and the extent of her personal liberty bore little resemblance to what Anne would be allowed to enjoy at a comparable age.

There may have been dreams of leading the life of an 'ordinary' child, but if the restrictions of some parts of her childhood irked Elizabeth at all she apparently experienced little or none of the frustration that made her daughter want to go to boarding school.

By modern standards it was a very limited existence but it was a very happy one for Elizabeth, growing up in the emotional environment her father had longed for and her mother had known, with the security of love, much laughter, an unrepressed companionship with her parents, and a salting of the fun and mischief she and Margaret contrived between themselves.

There was little to disturb the happiness of the York family until Elizabeth was ten and her father had to take on the unwanted responsibility of the monarchy. In 1931 King George had offered them Royal Lodge in Windsor Great Park as a country home. Owing to the national economic crisis that year the Duke of York, in line with the royal example, postponed any extensive repairs to the house, but directly the need for stringency passed he and the Duchess set to on the enjoyable pastime of making the kind of home they had dreamed of. Once it was ready Royal Lodge became the more permanent home, and, until the move to Buckingham Palace, Elizabeth and Margaret for a great deal of the time led the kind of country existence with dogs and ponies that the majority of children would envy.

In those years the Duke's public duties were expanding and he was becoming even more involved with his special interests – the field of industrial welfare and his annual camps for boys drawn from both industrial areas and public schools, first established in 1921. As second in the line of succession he was always ready to shoulder his share of royal engagements in addition to those undertaken in his own right, and he frequently represented the King overseas. And although still restricted by the King's narrow-minded refusal to give access to affairs of state to his second son, the Duke had been a Counsellor of State since his father's illness in 1928. But despite the busy life with public and social affairs, the Duke and Duchess always found time to enjoy the country pursuits in which they and their daughters delighted.

To forget the onus of protocol and immerse himself in the simple pleasures of home life and the countryside was always the Duke's idea of real enjoyment. As a young man he was a fine athlete and in the year Elizabeth was born he competed in the men's doubles at Wimbledon. Although his daughter did not share all her father's enthusiasm for games she certainly inherited the same instinctive 'way with a horse'. He gave her her first pony when she was four, a little Shetland called Peggy, which proved to be the originator of Elizabeth's love of ponies and horses.

In those days young children were not taught riding in the professional way that Princess Anne and her contemporaries enjoyed. Elizabeth was taught the rudiments by her parents, and her tuition was then handed into the safe-keeping of a family groom who saw to it that his charge knew such essentials as how to hold the reins, then attached a leading rein – a handbrake that he was reluctant to relinquish long after it was unnecessary – and took her out riding.

Before very long Elizabeth was able to accompany her father, and until his ill-health precluded the sport it was one of their great pleasures to ride together in the lovely surroundings of the Windsor parks. As soon as she was able, Margaret joined her sister in the riding, and early in 1936 they were given a short course of lessons by a qualified instructor.

Even as a child Elizabeth was not able to give as much time to riding as she would have liked but, typically, she got as much out of the lessons as she possibly could. To get to the root of a matter and really learn the why and wherefore is one of the Queen's strong character traits, and in those days she set out to learn whatever she could about pony management and welfare in addition to riding.

Both children inherited their father's sharp mind and his attractive sense of the ridiculous, but were otherwise unalike. The Queen's tranquillity comes from her mother, and when quite young she seemed to possess a down-to-earth common sense, the ability to work hard and a conscientiousness that developed with the years. She had, and has retained, something of her father's quick temper and a decided will of her own, but is the lucky possessor of an essentially happy nature. Elizabeth could be as gay as her more inconsequential sister, but there was always an underlying seriousness. She was receptive more than creative, and although only ten when her father became King, she seemed to have a precocious understanding and appreciation of the devotion to public service and the great sense of duty that ruled his life.

Margaret was the extrovert, volatile, vivacious, able to charm her father into helpless laughter even when he was annoyed with her. Both sisters enjoyed acting – the Queen often unconsciously displays her talent as a mimic when she is talking about someone – but it was Margaret who exhibited a brilliant aptitude for the same art, as well as an enviable ability to play the piano by ear.

Elizabeth could scarcely avoid becoming the true country-lover she is at heart. Her father's love and knowledge of the countryside and wild life went far deeper than the field sports that engendered them. Like King George V he was a first-class shot and found satisfaction in proving his marksmanship, but however the day was spent, in the butts, rough shooting, wild fowling, the size of the bag bore little relation to the overall enjoyment because his pleasure was rooted in a love of the land and the open air.

After his accession it was in the province of sport that he could relax, be among friends with whom he could 'put off the King' and talk the same language of forest and field. Because this perception of the countryside and all that it meant was no veneer but an element of the man himself, Elizabeth grew up in a world where it was a matter of course to spend every possible moment in the open air, regardless of weather. With her mother she learnt the peace, and the moments of excitement, of fishing for salmon in the brawling waters of the River Dee. As a family they were great ones for walking; tramping round the various estates they were always on the look-out for the enchanting red squirrels with light-coloured tails that flit up and down the trees at Balmoral, for the occasional golden eagle like the one Queen

Victoria noted 'towering splendidly above', for a glimpse of fox or badger. From her father Elizabeth learned the ways of the wild red deer, the lore of hare, woodcock and grouse. The wide reaches of sky and russet fields of Norfolk in winter became as familiar as the heather-covered hills round Balmoral, or the shining, delicate green of beech trees coming into leaf in the Windsor parks. She knew the sound of deep-channelled peaty burns on their way to the hustling river in the valley, the primeval silence before dawn that brings the first flight of wild duck.

Outside the secure happiness of Elizabeth's early childhood the world was boiling up for the cataclysms and catastrophes so soon to come. In 1930 the man-in-the-street was probably more concerned with the exploits of Don Bradman, the brilliant Australian cricketer who first brought a test team to Britain that year, than with the coming to power in the 'new' Germany of the National Socialist German Workers' Party, soon to be known as the Nazis, a name with more sinister connotations. By the mid-thirties Hitler was Chancellor of Germany, Japan had withdrawn from the League of Nations, Arab and Jew were killing each other in Palestine and Mussolini had invaded Abyssinia.

In England the ripples of anxiety over the King's health, first stirred by his serious illness in 1928, were sharpened by recurring bronchial trouble. By the spring of 1935 his immediate family knew that the King was failing.

As for Elizabeth herself, she had already met a young relative called Prince Philip of Greece when she was eight, and they were to meet again within the year at her father's coronation. But at this moment in time there was no reason for her knowing or remarking on the fact that Philip was a pupil at a boarding-school in Scotland.

Philip's childhood

PHILIP was born a Prince of Greece but is not of Greek blood. His grandfather William, a son of King Christian IX of Denmark, was nominated in 1863 by the European powers, and by Britain in particular, to take the throne of Greece and become George I of the Hellenes, and since then one or other of Philip's uncles and three cousins has, at various times, occupied that not over-stable Greek throne.

The uncle, Constantine I, who ruled from 1913 to 1917 and again from 1920 to 1922, was brother to Philip's father, His Royal Highness the Prince Andrew of Greece. Both were sons of George I, and all of them of the royal house of Denmark.

Through other lines of descent Philip can claim kinship with most, possibly all, the royal houses of Europe. By the complex ramifications of royal relationships he and the Queen are third cousins, sharing a common ancestry with, among others, Astrid, sister of the famous King Canute, and both are great-great-grandchildren of Queen Victoria. This line on Philip's side can be traced back through his mother, Princess Alice, who was one of Queen Victoria's great-granddaughters and a daughter of Louis, Prince of Battenberg, one-time British First Sea Lord, who was created first Marquess of Milford Haven, with the surname of Mountbatten, in 1917. Princess Alice, who was also a sister of Earl Mountbatten of Burma, died in 1969.

The Queen and Prince Philip also have a mutual link with the royal house of Denmark through their paternal great-grandfathers, King Christian IX, who had a proverbially lovely daughter, Alexandra, and King Edward VII, who married her.

Philip was Prince Andrew's only son and very much younger than his four sisters, an accident of birth that left him out of some, but by no means all, the family's early turbulent years. He was not born when Constantine succeeded to the throne after the assassination of George I in 1913, nor was he there four years later when King Constantine was forced to abdicate in favour of his son Alexander, and Philip's father shared his brother's exile.

On that occasion Prince Andrew took his family to Switzerland. He went back to Greece in 1920, and shared in some of the triumph connected with Constantine's return to the throne as the result of a plebiscite held after Alexander's sudden death. But despite the King's enthusiastic reception it was not the best of moments to have a young family of the royal blood in Athens, especially as Princess Alice was pregnant. The country was still bubbling with political unrest, the different factions united only in a common hatred of the Turks, and so Prince Andrew decided to take his wife and daughters and their English nanny to the island of Corfu. There they remained in the family villa, Mon Repos, while the Prince returned to his life of soldiering.

A clever, quick-witted and amusing man, Prince Andrew, true to the tradition of continental royal princes, had been schooled for the Army since he was seventeen and seen military service from the age of nineteen. In June 1921 he was appointed Major-General 2nd Army Corps, and took command at the front in Asia Minor against the Turks. His son, Philip, a strong, fair-haired baby, was born on 10 June.

Philip was only a few weeks old when Princess Alice brought the children to England so that she could attend the funeral of her father, Louis Mountbatten, Marquess of Milford Haven. They stayed at Netley Abbey, close to Broadlands, Earl Mountbatten of Burma's home in Hampshire, which Philip would one day know so well.

On their return to Greece the Princess found that her husband, sickened by the endless intrigue and general incompetence of all concerned with the Turkish campaign, had requested to be relieved of his command. He was still technically an Army officer, but rejoined his family on Corfu to live, as he believed, in peace.

Less than a year later Philip and his sisters were again in England with their mother, this time for the wedding of the Princess's brother, then Lord Louis Mountbatten, a ceremony from which Philip was excluded because of his youth.

This visit was curtailed by even more disturbing news from Greece. After much bloody fighting the Greeks had been routed by the Turks and the public mood was one of rage and national humiliation, the situation being exacerbated by the massacre and savage sacking and burning of Smyrna that followed. The Army mutinied, political power was seized by a revolutionary group and King Constantine again fled the country.

Prince Andrew had been promised an unmolested existence if he remained

Engagement, marriage and family

During the war Philip served with the navy. He is seen here in 1947 with a group of his fellow-officers

In the 1950s in Scotland, walking with a party of friends

Left At Euston Station on their way to Glasgow just after they became engaged

Right Philip's other great interest besides the sea was polo

Opposite In 1947 the engagement of Princess Elizabeth and
Lieutenant Mountbatten is formally announced

They were married in Westminster Abbey in November 1947

Prince Charles was born in 1948. No
smile for the photographer

One of the family occasions the
Queen and her husband have always
been anxious to preserve is the annual
holiday at Balmoral. With Charles
and Anne in 1952, and, more recently,
leaving Balmoral station

Eighteen months
later, in 1950,
Princess Anne was
born. The young
family are in the
grounds of Clarence
House, then their
London home

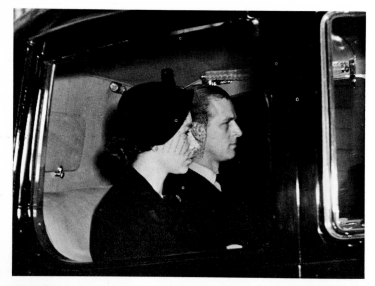

In February 1952, while Princess
Elizabeth and Prince Philip were in
Kenya, King George VI died and
they returned immediately to
take up the full burden of official
life

On the balcony at Buckingham Palace after the Coronation on 2 June 1953.
On Prince Philip's right are the Queen Mother and Princess Margaret; in the
foreground, Prince Charles and Princess Anne

in Corfu, but in October 1922 he was suddenly summoned to Athens. The pretext was for him to attend the court of the Revolutionary Committee as a witness against those charged with responsibility for the Greek defeat, but once in the capital he was arrested, imprisoned for seven weeks, and brought to trial on a trumped-up charge of treason.

Princess Alice, only too aware of the number of summary executions already implemented, appealed frantically for help to the Pope and foreign heads of state. In response King George v of England dispatched a light cruiser to the scene, with orders for her commander to make contact with those working desperately under cover to save Prince Andrew's life.

This intervention, with the aid of much delicate and secret diplomacy, resulted in the Prince's being pardoned, although he was indicted on the monstrously false accusation of abandoning his post in the face of the enemy, and 'degraded and condemned to perpetual banishment'. But he was allowed, again in the utmost secrecy, to rejoin his family, already on board HMS *Calypso* waiting off Phaleron.

They sailed for Brindisi, and from there the family made their way to Paris, that Mecca for the growing numbers of royal exiles, returning after a brief stay in England to settle at St Cloud, where they had the loan of a relative's house.

By 1926, the year in which Princess Elizabeth was born, Philip was a tough, active little boy of five, leading a life from which most of the royal trimmings had been stripped, but which was certainly not one of actual poverty. Certainly the family were part of a community where many, however aristocratic, were only too glad to earn their living in any way they could, be it driving a taxi or working as a waiter, and by previous standards Prince Andrew was not well off. But the English nanny remained part of the household, and although Princess Alice for a time ran a little shop in the rue du Faubourg St Honoré, the small proceeds from selling Greek handicrafts were not used to augment the family income but, typically, for helping infinitely needier Greek refugees. Equally, although Philip was brought up to appreciate the value of money, when he was urged to save up for some treasure such as a bicycle, it was more for the good of his soul than from actual economic necessity.

With a family composed of sisters, the youngest seven years older than himself, Philip might presumably have suffered from petticoat influence, particularly as his parents were no longer young and were to drift apart, his father going away about the time the last daughter married in 1931. Perhaps he did in fact suffer from such influence in an upside-down fashion, for the girls were so afraid of their little brother's being spoiled that they took hard-hearted pains to make sure he was not. Out of it all Philip began to emerge as a very boyish, sometimes pugnacious child, a bit of a show-off, with an over-abundance of energy and showing early promise of becoming a good athlete. He was always encouraged to be independent and self-reliant. He was friendly, and although lacking companions of his own age at home, had no trouble in finding plenty among the children of his mother's acquaintances and at the school he attended in St Cloud, where his classmates came mostly from families attached to the diplomatic corps.

During these years the children spent their holidays staying first with one and then with another of their innumerable relatives – on the Baltic Sea; at Sinaia with Queen Helen of Rumania and her young son Michael – or at Blakeney in Norfolk and, when their parents were in America, at Kensington Palace with their grandmother, the widowed Marchioness of Milford Haven.

Soon it was time to consider a boarding-school for Philip, and Princess Alice, her thoughts naturally turning to England, had little difficulty in persuading her husband that an English background offered more to a stateless prince than any other. On the advice of Princess Alice's brother, the second Marquess of Milford Haven, they sent their son to Cheam School, then near Newbury.

Philip quickly settled to the life of a typical prep-school boy, entering with enthusiasm into any sport or game going, and soon catching attention for his above-average abilities in these fields. He often spent the Christmas and Easter holidays at Lyndon Manor, a riverside house at Maidenhead belonging to the Marquess and, since he had no real roots in Paris and no remembrance of Greece, this really became Philip's home for a while. Here he had the company of his high-spirited cousin David, two years his senior, with whom he had a great deal of fun and got into the normal amount of boyish trouble.

If we add up the flying hours that Prince Philip puts in each year, it seems less surprising when he says that, given an entirely free choice, his career would have been with the RAF. But with a family tradition of the sea – although his father was an Army officer his grandfathers and uncles on both sides served with the Navy – it was perhaps the seafaring tales he heard at Lyndon Manor from his ex-sailor uncle, George, that first conditioned and then dedicated Philip to a naval career.

For some time he continued to spend the summer holidays at St Cloud, but although his mother did not return to Athens until 1937, the family was soon no longer a unit. All four sisters married in the years 1930 and 1931, all choosing German noblemen as husbands, and before long Philip was spending some of the holidays with one or other of them, usually in company with his father, cementing the affectionate bond between them. The marriage of the youngest sister was instrumental in sending Philip to Salem, a school in Germany that was founded by a man called Kurt Hahn.

This remarkable character had been secretary to Prince Max of Baden, the father-in-law of Philip's sister, Theodora, a man of philanthropic views, who had encouraged Hahn to found a progressive school, in 1917, in part of the enormous *Schloss* close to Lake Constance belonging to the Prince. Here fees were adjusted to the parents' income so that lack of money was no bar to entry, and the whole concept of the school was based on principles not at that time usually given priority in more conservative establishments. Hahn felt strongly that children should have the chance to find out from experience at an early age how to meet both triumph and defeat. His fee structure gave equal opportunity to boys of different backgrounds, and freed many pupils from what their headmaster considered the debilitating sense of privilege, too often conferred by birth on the sons of the wealthy and powerful.

Theodora's advocacy of Salem for her brother was influenced largely by her husband's connections with the school, but she also felt that it would make it easier for their mother, increasingly lonely with the years, to see more of Philip.

The family were convinced by her arguments and the English uncles acquiesced, but in the meantime Philip was thoroughly enjoying life at Cheam. He looked like an English boy, had acquired the English outlook, spoke the language without an accent, and except for an un-English fluency in French was in most ways a product of his country of adoption. The early promise at sport was being realized. In his last cricket season at prep-school, Philip was described as 'a greatly improved all-rounder and lively in the field'; he played soccer for the school, won the high-diving championship and shared first place in the under-twelves high jump. But although obviously intelligent, with a lively, quick mind and, as yet, an undeveloped artistic sense, Philip was not 'bookishly' inclined and his scholastic record was average.

ELIZABETH AND PHILIP

The inexhaustible energy and irrepressible sense of fun that remain so large a part of his character today landed Philip in most of the usual schoolboy scrapes and he was beaten on more than one occasion. Cheam found this boy both worthwhile and likeable, and his headmaster considered that he had a more than ordinary share of personality and leadership, two of the qualities most needed in high office. The regret was mutual when he left.

Philip arrived at Salem an untidy, tousle-headed twelve-year-old with a friendly grin and a broken front tooth – since remedied – the result of a roller-skating collision with his cousin David. In the beginning his German was sketchy, which did not make life any easier. Kurt Hahn was absent, recently removed as an involuntary 'guest' of the Nazis, and these and other aspects of life in Germany combined with the reluctance to leave Cheam to make that year at Salem about the only time in his life Philip has not enjoyed.

This was 1933, the year Hitler took office as German Chancellor, but there were few in Britain to understand the implications. Many cherished the illusion that a peaceful future with Germany was perfectly feasible, Hitler or no Hitler. This view was strengthened by belief in the new Chancellor's promises, including those contained in his speech to the Reichstag that year, when he promised total German disarmament.

Already Hitler's Brownshirts were indulging in Jew-baiting and worse, and many Jews, including numbers of intellectuals, had fled the country. The signs of ill-omen were clearly visible. The Nazis were not yet absolute masters of Germany, Hitler not yet dictator, but even at Salem Hahn's all-pervading humanitarian views seemed to be infiltrated by an indefinable, alien sense of regimentation. The headmaster himself had been arrested by the Gestapo and gaoled, cynically, for the 'decadent corruption of German youth'. It was an inevitable fate for one of such well-known liberal views, for when storm-troopers trampled a man to death not far from the school, Hahn assembled the boys to tell them they must choose between Salem philosophy and that of Nazism. He was extricated and allowed to leave the country only after worldwide appeals to President Hindenburg, and with the direct intervention of the British Prime Minister, Ramsay MacDonald.

Young as he was, anything of the Nazi doctrine that Philip gleaned was detestable to his way of thinking, a viewpoint that he made no attempt to hide. Apart from other considerations he thought all the heel-clicking and saluting ludicrous and made endless fun of these outward signs of pseudo-military might, refusing point-blank to consider using the Nazi salute when it was made a compulsory form of greeting. One way and another it seemed to Philip's family that it would be better and safer for all concerned if he returned to England.

Philip was delighted. Already he was looking at life through English eyes, and this time he was to base himself on England for good. He arrived in the autumn of 1934, to come under the care of his Uncle George, and into new and complete contact with the man and form of education most likely to develop his qualities.

With the help and encouragement of people as influential and diverse as the late Lord Tweedsmuir, the Archbishop of York, and C. A. Elliott, the then headmaster of Eton, Kurt Hahn had started up again with a school in Scotland. He was established at Gordonstoun House in remote, rugged countryside close by the Moray Firth, surroundings ideally suited to producing 'complete men with practised hands and alert, cultivated minds'. Here to join the thirty or so boys who made up the full complement of the newly founded school came the young Prince Philip of Greece.

In those first years there were none of the tennis and squash courts, certainly not the heated swimming-pool that Prince Charles and his 390 schoolmates were to enjoy in their time. And the hockey and cricket matches at which, although he insists it was because there was little choice, Philip eventually captained the school teams, were always 'away' fixtures owing to a total lack of school playing-fields. They were part of the dreams of the future, not as far distant as the science blocks and impressive sports hall of today, not quite as urgent as the extra dormitories, and the pig-sty, that Philip and his friends helped to bring into being.

Unlike more conventional public schools Gordonstoun is not obsessive about organized games and offers a number of athletic alternatives. Full use is made of the specially chosen amenities of mountains and sea to broaden boys' minds, train their initiative and imagination and help keep their bodies fit and strong. But there is also a rare, sensitive understanding of spiritual requirements such as the healing provided by solitude and silence. The school is not, and never has been, the regimented establishment of the spartan, body-building cult it has sometimes been made out to be by the unknowing.

One of the Gordonstoun ideals is to provide boys with the psychological and physical environment in which to 'discover their own powers', at whatever level, and of all those who have been through the school and made such a discovery, few can have been better equipped to take full advantage of the adventure than Prince Philip. Years later his son was also to 'find himself' at Gordonstoun, but because he has in many ways a different, more gentle personality, the going was harder for Charles.

Not that Philip was, or is, a paragon of patience. He has never suffered fools gladly, and if his temper is quickly over it is equally quick to flare. At times Kurt Hahn found him impatient, hasty in his judgements and intolerant. It is said that Philip learned to ride a horse at Gordonstoun 'under orders', for scoffing at others who enjoyed an interest he did not at that time share. But as his headmaster soon noted: 'Philip's most remarkable trait was his undefeatable spirit.'

He was always and remains a two-hundred-per-center, incapable of doing anything by halves, even when it came to feeling happy or sad. Once his interest was aroused Philip would take over any project, from building a boat to organizing one of the school's community aid schemes, and make it his own, paying meticulous attention to every detail. He took enormous pride in good workmanship, and mediocrity was and remains something unknown to him. He took pride, too, in being physically hard and fit, one good reason for enjoying polo, and proved fearless, especially in or on the water. Even in those days Philip was demonstrating an inherent dislike of personal publicity, but would then co-operate in situations such as the cricket match against the village, when a posse of girl autograph-hunters requested signatures from all the school team – and the master in charge reckoned it would save time and trouble if Philip alone complied!

Ask anyone who knows Prince Philip well for his most characteristic trait and they will give the same answer: his genuine kindness of heart that he does his best to conceal. There are numbers of people around today who are thankful for the time, thought and trouble that one of the busiest of men tries, whenever possible, to give to other people's problems.

As a five-year-old he demonstrated an instinctive and, for his age, exceptional thoughtfulness, by handing over all his toys to an invalid child, omitted by an obtuse adult from the general present-giving. Years later when a lady visitor, returning to Gordonstoun from a muddy walk, found a bunch of boys cleaning their shoes outside the building she asked for the loan of a brush. It was Philip who immediately took command of the situation. 'Put one foot . . . there . . ., and the other foot . . . there . . . and then see what happens!' he said, an act of such in-born kindness and good manners that the recipient of his shoe-shining efforts asked if she could repay in kind.

Philip promptly inquired if she could darn, because he was 'ashamed of his football stockings'!

During the Gordonstoun era Philip much enjoyed those holidays spent in Germany with one or other of his sisters and, usually, with his father. Father and son were much alike in looks, sharing the same mannerisms and the way they moved and stood. They much appreciated and enjoyed each other's company, and when it comes to the laughter that bubbles up at the least expected moments, to the fun that Philip extracts from life, from situations and from himself, these again are legacies from Prince Andrew and his Danish ancestry. The streak of obstinacy that runs through Philip's nature was present in both parents, but he is lucky in also having inherited the dogged persistence and drive that sustained his mother, and carried her through all the turmoils and tragedies of her long life.

In those days and for some years to come Prince Philip was still in line of succession to the Greek throne, a circumstance of which his mother had been fully aware when her son was born, and one that Prince Andrew did not allow him to forget. The fact was highlighted by the restoration of the Greek monarchy in 1935, and a year later by a royal reunion for a family funeral in Athens that Philip attended.

He himself accepted his standing as a fact of life, a remote possibility that made little difference except to prove, sometimes, more of a disadvantage than a blessing. He has always been far more concerned with the man than with the prince, and even had he been the type to be markedly aware of his status, Gordonstoun would soon have remedied the tendency. At the school he worked and played with boys from many different backgrounds, and found a number of friends among the fishermen and their families who lived in the nearby hamlet of Hopeman.

During his school years some of Philip's penchant for 'messing about in boats' was perhaps, as he avers, to avoid the footslogging he had so loathed at Salem. Nevertheless the sea had the same powerful attraction for him that it still exerts, and he spent every available moment consciously or unconsciously assimilating the fund of nautical lore that was to stand him in good stead in the future.

Kurt Hahn was 'spot on' when he assessed Philip's best as outstanding, his second-best as not good enough. His has always been a temperament that needs to be stretched to its limits. This is something that the Prince is fully aware of himself, that the Queen, who stopped trying to prevent him doing things years ago, understands and accepts, and that his personal staff who undertake his day-to-day arrangements and activities do their best to cope with.

Prince Philip is one of those born to lead, and the whole concept of Gordonstoun might have been created for the enlargement and fulfilment of just such a personality. It may have been chance that landed him at such a school, but it was neither chance nor prestige that made his schoolmates elect him Guardian or head boy. That is an honour achieved strictly on merit, in the same way that Philip qualified for the valued award of the King's Dirk as best cadet of his term at Dartmouth, and won the Eardley-Howard-Crockett prize as the best all-rounder – just as he was to gain a high pass mark for entry into the Royal Navy.

Philip entered Dartmouth College as a naval cadet in May 1939, a few weeks before he was eighteen and not many months before the outbreak of war. The Marquess of Milford Haven had died the previous year and by the request of Prince Andrew the younger uncle, Lord Louis Mountbatten, now assumed the same role of unofficial guardian.

About that time there had been some pressure from Greek circles to send the Prince to the Greek Nautical College, but Prince Andrew was as adamant as his son. Except by birth Philip was an Englishman, his career lay with the British Navy, and his twelve years with the service were to provide invaluable experience when it came to creating the unique job that he continues to expand.

That same year and only a week or two before Philip went to Dartmouth, Princess Elizabeth was riding in Windsor Park with her father, as the enjoyable start to her thirteenth birthday. The press photographs of the time show Elizabeth and Margaret as two nice-looking, rather solemn little girls. Margaret was only nine, and there was nothing of the modern sophisticated teenager about her elder sister. Children did not then grow up as quickly as they do today, and juvenile clothing styles kept them strictly to (or below) their age-group. On the other hand, in a photograph taken about this time at a fancy-dress party given by Viscountess Astor, Elizabeth, with her elegant medieval hair-style and becoming full-length gown, could be a youthfully dignified fifteen.

However, it was the child of thirteen whom Philip met in July that year, when the King took his family on the royal yacht *Victoria and Albert* to make his first visit to Dartmouth since leaving the College twenty-six years previously.

PHILIP'S CHILDHOOD

Lord Louis Mountbatten was also on board as naval ADC to the King, and his presence, combined with the fact that his nephew was a royal relative anyway, ensured Philip's meeting the family. But before he and the other cadet captains dined on the royal yacht, a party that was for adults only and recalled as very enjoyable, it is an undisputed fact that he and Elizabeth met for the third time in their lives. The details vary, but since an outbreak of chicken-pox amongst the cadets had confined the Princesses, on shore, to the precincts of the captain's house, it seems reasonable that Philip should have been detailed to entertain them for the afternoon. Where the romantics embark on flights of pure fancy is in suggesting that this meeting was when Philip decided he was going to marry the future Queen!

Philip was a gay, attractive young man of eighteen just embarking on a career where he was determined to leave his mark. There was nothing of the gauche teenager about him, his cosmopolitan connections had seen to that, and his independence and self-sufficiency were added attractions. Not surprisingly he was already a success on the social scene, his impact, even as a schoolboy, on the younger set in Venice the previous year proving the point. But he was not of an age or inclination, or in the circumstances, to give romance, let alone the scarcely considered possibility of marriage at some dim, far-off date, a thought more serious than on the delightful, light-hearted level of flirtation; and Elizabeth was far too young for that.

One story goes to the other extreme and suggests that Philip was distinctly put out at having to entertain the two girls at all, but that seems as far fetched as the 'sudden romance' version.

Where Elizabeth was concerned it may have been a little different. She was not too young to have a hero; there cannot have been many young men of Philip's age and charm among her acquaintances, and what girl could resist thinking, and maybe dreaming, about such an attractive, lively personality as that dashing naval cadet?

Britain at war

PRINCESS ELIZABETH was in Scotland on that Sunday, 3 September 1939, when the air-raid sirens in London and throughout much of England started wailing almost as Mr Chamberlain, the Prime Minister, finished delivering the declaration of war.

It had been an odd summer, the hot, sunny days overhung with a sense of foreboding and uncertainty, yet the beaches and resorts were crowded with holiday-makers apparently carefree in spite of the gas-masks tucked in among their baggage. Preparations for war were going forward on a national scale, but the idea of war was so unthinkable to the majority of people in Britain that they clung to an innate optimism, feeling that if only events could somehow stagger through the autumn without actually exploding, all must yet be well.

The King shared the same hope, differently expressed, his sensitive nature refusing to contemplate the outcome if Hitler, after all, did not have second thoughts.

The royal family had been spending their usual summer holiday at Balmoral, making the most of the weeks of sunshine, the King more than usually embroiled in what turned out to be the last of his 'Duke of York's Camps', acting as camp chief to the two hundred boys under canvas in the grounds of nearby Abergeldie Castle.

That year camp competitions had been dropped in favour of expeditions, and each day the King set off with a different group of boys, who were mostly city-bred, tramping for miles as he showed them the lovely countryside he had known from childhood and the equally familiar wild life that inhabited it. It proved an informal and rewarding companionship, and one shared to a small degree by Elizabeth and Margaret, who helped to make the boys feel happy and relaxed when they came to tea at Balmoral. On the last night of the camp, when the flames of the traditional huge bonfire were spiking the outer darkness where Balmoral pipers marched and played, the sisters were there with their parents, joining in the singing until the last notes of 'Auld Lang Syne' brought an end to the camp, and, symbolically, almost an end to the peace.

ELIZABETH AND PHILIP

On 22 August came the announcement of the Soviet-German Pact of Non-Aggression. It stunned the Allies and sent the King hurrying to London to join his ministers, knowing with an agonized certainty that for the second time in his life the country was to be at total war.

By the middle of that September the war at sea, with the sinking of the *Athenia* and the aircraft carrier *Courageous*, had claimed almost seven hundred casualties, and only a month later the *Royal Oak* was torpedoed in Scapa Flow. But in British towns and villages, despite the blackout and rationing, the evacuation of the children and closing of places of entertainment, those first months were somehow comparable to that first air-raid warning. True, that had proved a false alarm while the state of war unfortunately remained a grim reality, but the inaction on land at that time produced an unreal period of suspended animation, soon dubbed the 'phoney war'. It proved a heaven-sent breathing space, but as the weeks went by with nothing much happening on the French front and a total absence of bombing at home, let alone the expected blitz, people were lulled into a dangerous complacency, even to the point of bringing back their children to the built-up areas.

There was some truth in the German propaganda assertion that the royal children were to be sent to Canada for the duration. The idea was discussed at one point as a matter that concerned the safety and survival of the Heiress Presumptive, but the King and Queen were adamant. With the great majority of their people, they felt it only right they should face what was to come together, and from a personal angle the thought of splitting the family appalled them. Obviously precautions were taken. Wherever possible everyone was being urged to keep children out of key towns and cities. The Princesses stayed on in Scotland until Christmas that first year, and when they came south they went to Windsor. In the ensuing years there was the occasional holiday at Balmoral, but except for the odd day now and again Elizabeth and Margaret stayed out of London until the last stages of the war.

In Scotland they continued the normal routine of lessons with their governess, and while the hot days of summer soon acquired a tang of autumn and then faded out into early winter, every free moment was as usual spent outside in the grounds. Life at the Castle proceeded at its accustomed un-flurried pace, with few differences except for one unexpected bonus brought about by the skeleton staff kept on in royal service throughout the war. There was no one to spare as full-time groom for the children's ponies, so with the minimum of supervision and with much enjoyment and satisfaction they took on the main part of the job themselves.

The inscription on the back of a photograph of a lively looking pony is written in the Queen's hand and reads: 'Jock – who taught me more than any other horse.' But that bronze-coloured animal of unpredictable ways did more than teach his young rider how to look after a pony on her own. Jock and Hans, the smaller animal of Scandinavian extraction that belonged to Margaret, provided the sisters with a new, exciting freedom, more extensive than any they had known. For the first time in their lives they could, within reason, saddle up and ride when and where they liked, coping by themselves with all the inevitable mishaps that befall children and ponies everywhere, and out on their own among the heather and hills of the estate except for a policeman on a bicycle, toiling far off along one of the tracks.

After Christmas, spent at Royal Lodge in Windsor Park, the King and Queen returned to Buckingham Palace where, except for short periods and the time they could snatch with their daughters, they remained in residence throughout the war.

The life that Elizabeth spent at Windsor, particularly during the first year or two, was, from the social angle, very quiet and uneventful, the same kind of existence that many girls of her age were leading at the time. There was the occasional happening, like the nativity play at the Park School, put on by children of the King's tenants at Christmas 1940, in which the Princesses took part. As they grew older one or two small informal dances were held for them, but otherwise there was little social life, and most of the time not taken up with actual lessons was spent in reading or sketching, riding or driving the ponies and walking and playing with the dogs.

But if Elizabeth's activities were not exactly out of the ordinary, her knowledge of current affairs certainly was. Important affairs of state are not discussed with anyone, let alone a child, but after her father's accession Elizabeth's studies in constitutional history became considerably more concrete than abstract. She was there, in the centre of it all, and although young she inevitably became caught up in the national events that were, in a way, part of her own day-to-day life and that of those around her.

At the time, as a child of ten, it is unlikely that she would have been told or gleaned much of the detail that led to her uncle's abdication and her own father's becoming King. But children are acutely sensitive to the atmosphere of the adult world even if they do not understand it, and Elizabeth must have been conscious of her father's unhappiness and strain during those weeks leading up to the events that changed their world so drastically.

Soon, even before the upheaval of the move to Buckingham Palace had settled into perspective, Elizabeth's role had taken on new dimensions. As Heiress Presumptive she had to appear more often in public with the King and Queen, and quite apart from the routine functions, affairs and happenings that would be of no interest or moment to other children of her age became part of her existence. When war came she was only thirteen and a half, but because of her position that again meant a comprehension of the overall picture, unimaginable to the majority of young girls.

The 'phoney war' ended in the spring of 1940 with the German invasion of Denmark and Norway, and the subsequent failure of the British and French Norwegian campaign. Daily the news grew worse – Holland, Belgium, Luxembourg were invaded, and then came the grim, magnificent days of the evacuation of the British Army from France through Dunkirk, and the following weeks when the German forces crouched in the Channel ports waiting to invade. That cloudless autumn Elizabeth watched the criss-crossed vapour trails of the aerial dog-fights that latticed the sky, each pattern marking the boundaries of a new skirmish in the Battle of Britain. Soon her grasp of the war scene was to become even more personal.

The bombing had begun earlier with small-scale attacks before France capitulated, and by mid-August these were stepped up into the heavy assaults on the south-coast ports. The onslaught on London started on 7 September and two days later a bomb fell on Buckingham Palace. It did not go off on impact but later shattered the windows of the royal apartments. Less than a week later two bombs exploded in the quadrangle only thirty yards from the King's room, and he and the Queen had a frighteningly narrow escape. In all the Palace was hit nine times, but it was only for a short period during the fiercest of the bombing that the King and Queen could be persuaded to sleep at Windsor and return to Buckingham Palace to work each day.

A bomb fell in the vicinity of Windsor station, very close to the Castle, and two other small ones exploded on the Castle golf-course. Since Windsor is only twenty-three miles from the capital, night after night Elizabeth could see London's outline distorted by flames, and feel the reverberations of explosions powerful enough to shake even the eight-hundred-year-old walls of the Castle. Consciously or not she must have known the complete sense of unity that bound King and nation in those years, soon even to the extent of personal loss. For in 1942 Elizabeth and Margaret were with their parents at Balmoral when the news was received that the Duke of Kent, the King's youngest brother, had been killed on active service when the Sunderland flying boat carrying him to a mission in Iceland crashed into a Scottish mountainside during bad weather.

Maybe it was the result of a communal spirit that can be fully understood only by those who lived through the Second World War, but as the King travelled indefatigably up and down the country, visiting and cheering on fighter pilots, bomber crews, naval units, defence corps and assault troops; as he and the Queen went round London and the provincial towns and cities after the raids, to see and talk to the people on the spot in each devastated area; when, in the later stages, the King flew thousands of miles to inspect and inspire our armies overseas, he forged a bond such as the monarchy had never known before. He was the focus of the spirit of the times; but there was more to it than that. King, Queen, docker, tradesman, fireman, housewife, all were in it together.

Meanwhile Prince Philip, who had passed out of Dartmouth in 1940, had been posted as midshipman in the battleship *Ramillies,* on escort duty in the Indian Ocean. This was one of several appointments devised, for all his own frustration, to keep a royal prince of a neutral country serving with the British Navy, out of the battle zone where his capture, injury or demise could have been something more than an embarrassment. The policy was soon unnecessary, for the Italian invasion of Greece in October 1940 destroyed Philip's technical neutrality, and within a short while he was, and remained, on the operational scene. In the meantime he had been trying to remedy the situation by becoming a British subject, a status essential to a permanent commission in the Royal Navy, but the necessary legal machinery was not available during the war, and for various reasons, some connected with his kinship with the Greek King, Philip did not achieve British citizenship until 1947.

Once he was operational, Philip soon saw plenty of action. He was only nineteen and still a midshipman when he was given the Greek War Cross of Valour for the same 'efficiency in carrying out orders', during the rout of the Italian fleet at the battle of Cape Matapan in March 1941, that earned him a mention in dispatches. Three months earlier, and only three days after joining HMS *Valiant,* he had been in the naval bombardment of Bardia on the Libyan coast, with lively operations off Sicily following quickly after. In May that year the *Valiant* was heavily involved with the destroyer and cruiser squadrons to the north of Crete, in the costly but successful efforts to intercept the German seaborne landings.

By June Philip was back in England to work for his sub-lieutenant's examination, and that was when he started visiting the royal family for part of some of his leaves.

Elizabeth was then fifteen, Philip twenty. They liked each other and were good friends, he made her laugh, and if he happened to be around for any of those informal dances no doubt they danced together for a proportion of the evening, to their mutual enjoyment. Several times Philip was at Windsor for Christmas, including 1942 when his cousin David Milford-Haven was also of the party, and their uninhibited and noisy appreciation of the pantomime *Aladdin* contributed towards the overall success of one of the Princesses' annual productions.

From Queen Mary down to the youngest Kent cousin, all the family found Philip excellent company, and apart from other aspects of his cheerful presence, the King, as an ex-serving naval officer, took a lot of pleasure in the usually lighthearted accounts of wartime life in the senior service.

When Philip went back to sea he and Elizabeth started writing to each other occasionally, but there was nothing of the story-book romance about it. Philip, anyway, was far too busy with his career to spare a thought for anything more serious than 'girl friends', and he was too young himself to consider in that light anyone five years younger still. It might have been different, as Prince Philip says himself, it *could* have been highly significant if he had been someone completely outside the family, but he was not. The visits, the hospitality and correspondence came into the natural order of friendliness, extended to and enjoyed by a very likeable young relative who came home from the sea at intervals, and possessed no particular home ties of his own.

That is how it appears to Prince Philip in retrospect, and possibly that is how it appeared to a family no better or worse than any other at assessing the feelings of a young girl they still, in most respects, looked on as a child. Few knew what 'Lilibet', as they call her, at fifteen, at sixteen, at seventeen was thinking about it all, but it seems an odds-on bet that the occasional appearances of her attractive young third cousin were the highlights of those times.

With his aptitude, temperament and schooling, Philip could scarcely help

Duties dominate their lives

After the Trooping the Colour on the Queen's
official birthday in June

Combining duty with
pleasure: arriving at Royal
Ascot

Derby Day is another
permanent fixture for the
Queen and Prince Philip

On another occasion, even
the rain cannot spoil the
fashion parade for the
Queen and her daughter

State Occasions account for
a large part of the Queen's
and Prince Philip's life:
above, walking to the
Scottish General Assembly
in Edinburgh dressed
in the robes of the
Order of the Thistle

The Queen, Prince Philip
and all their children in
full evening dress for a
formal engagement

The investiture of the Prince of Wales at Caernaervon; a tense,
as well as a joyful occasion for the Queen

One of the many garden parties at Buckingham Palace given specially for people who have made a particular contribution to the life of the country. Among the royal guests on this occasion are members of the St John's Ambulance Brigade

Official engagements are not, of course, restricted to London. Shortly after Prince Charles's birth Princess Elizabeth and Prince Philip visited the Macclesfield silk mills where his christening robe was made

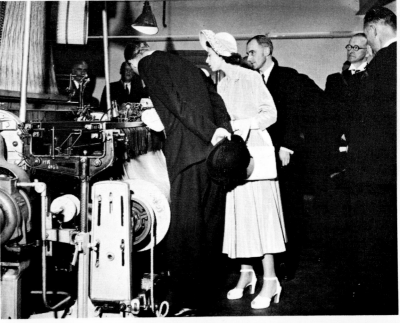

The Queen and Prince
Philip at the Highland game
pause for a few words with
piper

Prince Philip chatting and
joking with local inhabitant
the Shetland Isles, while the
Queen inspected a lifeboat c
on the first visit made by a
reigning monarch since 126

On an official visit to the University of Wales at Cardiff, Prince Philip drops in on a wedding party on the spur of the moment

When the new underground Victoria Line was opened in March 1969, the Queen drove it from Green Park to Oxford Circus

An unexpected encounter
sometimes interrupts the
formality of a state visit

Much to the lorry-drivers'
surprise, the Queen joined in
their tea-break when she was
driving along the M62
motorway shortly after it was
opened

being a success as a naval officer, whether in a war- or peace-time navy. The increasing responsibilities expanded his gift for leadership, and the technological and scientific skills demanded in a modern service gave him a grounding in the knowledge that forms the basis of many of his interests today. As a naval officer he grew up, enjoyed himself, found purpose, impressed others with his potential and was well liked by his contemporaries, senior officers and those who came under his command.

During the twelve years of his naval service there were many, as there still are, to find Philip's gay enthusiasm for life irresistible. The one who proved a completely kindred spirit, with the same tastes, same outlook, same naval ambitions, same laugh-at-life attitude topping the underlying seriousness, was an Australian. The friendship began when Philip's seniority, the outcome of a high rating in his sub-lieutenant examination results, made him at twenty-one, as first lieutenant in the destroyer *Wallace*, one of the youngest seconds-in-command in the British Navy. And when, characteristically, he set out to make his ship the most efficient in the squadron, he came into competition with Mike Parker, his opposite number in *Lauderdale,* of like intent and also on the same convoy work battling up and down the east coast between Rosyth and Sheerness.

He and Philip were to continue the friendly rivalry and satisfying friendship when their destroyers, Philip's *Whelp* and Mike's *Wessex,* were with the 27th Destroyer Flotilla of the Pacific Fleet in 1944–5. And in the future, when Elizabeth and Philip were married, Michael Parker was to become their equerry and friend, remaining with Philip as private secretary after Elizabeth became Queen, until he decided for personal reasons to relinquish the post in 1957.

While Philip had been seeing action at sea, first as a midshipman and then with increasing seniority, the war on all fronts had been continuing with landmarks, some dark and terrible, some shining with hope, that pointed the road, however obscurely at times, leading eventually to its end. In 1941 the German offensive into Russia secured the Soviet Union as an ally, and the Japanese attack on Pearl Harbor brought America into the war. In 1942 the loss of Singapore and other disasters in the Pacific went along with renewed bombing at home, some of it the savage retaliatory raids on undefended British cities. But the year continued with victory at Alamein, and the great defence of Stalingrad as the culmination of the Communist Army offensive. By 1943 the optimism of the High Command would be sufficient, if premature, for the King to be noting in his diary: 'Let us hope next Christmas will see the end of the war.'

In the spring of 1944, while Philip was busying himself in the Pacific seeing that *Wallace* kept her place as crack ship of the squadron, Elizabeth celebrated her eighteenth birthday.

Although she was the same age as her great-great-grandmother Victoria had been when she came to the throne, there were still three years to go before the Princess would be officially eligible as a Counsellor of State. She was, however, already starting to play her part in public life, and the King was determined that, unlike himself, his daughter should be prepared for every aspect of the exacting duties that must one day be hers. This included a thorough and increasing insight into affairs of state.

To this end Parliament had already amended the Regency Act, and when the King flew to visit his forces in Italy in the summer of 1944, for the first time Princess Elizabeth, with the Duke of Gloucester, the Princess Royal and Princess Arthur of Connaught, was appointed to act as Counsellor of State with her mother, the Queen.

Twenty-five years later Princess Anne, then also eighteen and just embarking on her own public duties, was to consider herself lucky in having what she called 'a gentle introduction' with a first official engagement with the Army. The King had appointed her mother Colonel-in-Chief of the Grenadier Guards at the age of sixteen, but it was on 26 April 1944 when she was eighteen that Princess Elizabeth attended a special 'birthday parade' of her regiment, to receive the Colonel's Standard, her own banner to be used on future inspections at the Changing of the Guard in the quadrangle at Windsor Castle.

Apart from the military ceremony and the family lunch that followed, Elizabeth spent the remainder of her birthday quietly. But in many parts of the country the crucial preparations for 'D' Day, the plan called 'Operation Overlord' for the invasion of Europe, were going forward steadily and in the utmost secrecy.

June approached and the tension heightened. The vital secrets of landing beaches and exact date were well kept, most of the brilliantly staged 'red herrings' to deceive the enemy successfully put over, but a full-blooded gale defeated the selected day of 5 June. It was twenty-four hours later that the packed landing craft and all the other ships of the four-thousand-strong invasion fleet at last set sail for France, under skies continually swept by an 'umbrella' of fighter planes and bombers.

Both the King and his Prime Minister had set their hearts on watching the invasion in person from some suitable ship of the line. It had taken much tactful and strong persuasion, and in the case of Winston Churchill eventually what amounted to a royal command, to steer first the King and then the Prime Minister away from a course that at national level could be seen only as unjustifiably hazardous. And so, at a moment when reason prevailed against the instincts of a man who always longed to be 'in the thick of it' with his people, the King joined his family and the nation in watching from afar and praying.

By 8 June, with the first tense days safely accomplished, it was clear that the landings and assault were successful. That evening the King broadcast to the nation, calling for a 'vigil of prayer' to further an enterprise that should end in liberation and peace. By the sixteenth the King was at last able to fulfil his ambition, and he went to the Normandy beaches to see the happenings and conditions for himself.

The King returned to Portsmouth that same night and went straight to Windsor, so that with her mother and sister Elizabeth was able to hear a first-hand account of the most stirring and crucial combined services operation ever undertaken. No doubt there was also discussion of the new threat at home, Hitler's first 'secret weapon'.

Only two nights previously the first wave of flying bombs had come clanking in over the Channel, dagger-shaped dark splodges against the darker sky, with flames pumping from their entrails and an inhuman infallibility about their pilotless flight that depressed public morale more than the worst of the bombing. During the first fortnight about 600 'doodlebugs' fell in the London area alone, killing 1,600 people, wounding a further 10,000 and damaging over 200,000 homes. Like most London buildings the windows of Buckingham Palace were so frequently blown in or sucked out by blast in the following weeks that they were replaced with wooden casements, the 'panes' made of talc.

Apart from a length of boundary wall demolished when a 'doodle' exploded in Constitution Hill, the Palace was not hit, but for a while the King and his Prime Minister were persuaded to eat their weekly luncheon together in the air-raid shelter. The royal family's shock at the destruction of the Guards' Chapel at Wellington Barracks was the deeper for losing personal friends and acquaintances among the casualties.

There was still Hitler's second 'vengeance weapon' to be endured, but only

1,250 faster-than-sound V2 rockets arrived in the country to create further devastation before all the sites and launching pads for both types of bomb, not already destroyed, were overrun by the advancing Allied armies. The end of the war in Europe was now clearly in sight.

Some months before Hitler's death and the final capitulation, Elizabeth had realized one of her dearest ambitions. Conforming to wartime regulations she had registered for National Service when she was sixteen, but despite her pleadings to join one of the women's services or to do some regular war work she had been unable to persuade her father to agree. Then at last, early in 1945, the King granted his elder daughter a commission, with the honorary rank of Second Subaltern, in the ATS, the first woman member of the royal family to join as a full-time, active member of the services. However, her increasing public commitments meant that the appointment could only be a brief one – Elizabeth relinquished her commission with the Honorary rank of Brigadier on her accession – but there were by-products.

Elizabeth was posted to No. 1 Mechanical Transport Training Centre where she was in frequent daily contact with young people of many different types. This was a big help to a girl who was shy and retiring by nature and who because of the war, had grown up in more than ordinary royal seclusion. Like her husband and children the Queen is mechanically minded. Maybe that course in driving, car maintenance and repair has something to do with the fact that she handles a car with above-average expertise, and although she drives only in the privacy of the royal estates, if the occasion demands it she can demonstrate the same liking for speed as her family. This 'bent' of the Queen's might account for Anne's ambition, at one stage, to take a course in engineering.

The end of the war came at last and after five long terrible years victory in Europe was formally announced and celebrated on VE-Day, 8 May 1945. The country did not go wild with joy as it had on that Armistice Day twenty-seven years before. Maybe it was difficult to realize that it really was the end, and anyway the war was still continuing in the Pacific. But in London the people flocked in their thousands to Buckingham Palace, shouting for their King, the man and his family who had been through it all with them. Their demands brought the King and Queen and Princesses out on to the Palace balcony eight times during that afternoon and evening.

Elizabeth would never forget those scenes and the pride she felt for her father. Nor would she and Margaret forget how later that evening he entrusted them to the care of some young officer friends and they slipped out and down among the crowds jammed into Whitehall and the Mall, to savour for themselves the exhilarating feel and taste and sound of the mass emotions of thankfulness and joy.

Prince Philip celebrated VE-Day a little later, on the other side of the world, when *Whelp* put in at Melbourne. When the King and his family were again sharing the reactions of the crowds packed in front of Buckingham Palace to celebrate VJ-Day, Victory over Japan on 2 September 1945, Prince Philip was with *Whelp* in Tokyo Bay.

Romance and engagement

THE victory parade was held over until June the following year, and once the immediate end-of-war celebrations were over the country and its new Socialist Government settled down to assess, and attempt to solve, some of the pressing problems of the peace.

The King was tired, drained physically and mentally by the exhausting stresses of the war that followed so quickly on the heels of his unwanted and precipitate accession. He longed for the unattainable, to get right away from people and functions, from protocol and responsibilities and the unrelenting flow of state papers. Even the Christmas holiday at beloved Sandringham with his family, the first to be spent in the big house since 1940, did little to restore his nervous energies, and for one so dedicated to duty there was to be little respite in the years to come.

Since her first emergence in 1944, Elizabeth's public life had been increasing. Sometimes she would be with the King and Queen, helping with official functions at the Palace, on a two-day visit to Wales or watching a demonstration of gliders and airborne troops. By that time she was accustomed to being out on her own; familiarity had removed any nervousness from occasions such as inspecting her own battalion of the Grenadier Guards. In that July she acquired both her own royal coat of arms and a personal lady-in-waiting.

The King was determined that Elizabeth should be familiar with it all; the public was insatiable, and Elizabeth herself was anxious to do everything she could, and not only because it was invaluable training for a distant future she accepted as inevitable, even though she would not have chosen it. With such a close family relationship she could not fail to realize how the King had been drained of his reserves of never very robust strength, and she was only too glad to take on anything she could to relieve the burden. Between March and August 1946, among other commitments, Elizabeth accompanied her parents on seven official occasions. By herself she launched ships (HMS *Eagle,* then the biggest aircraft carrier in the world, at Belfast and a tanker in Sunderland); took the salute at marches past (the Army Cadet Force, and eight thousand Rangers in Hyde Park); opened public institutions; attended the commissioning service of the battleship *Vanguard* at Greenock; received an honorary degree of Bachelor of Music at London University; and was invested as a bard at the Welsh National Eisteddfod.

But if life had its increasingly serious side for her there was plenty of fun and laughter to spice it, and by that time a secret thought had begun to hold a very bright question mark for the future.

Food was still scarce; the fat ration was actually reduced in February 1946 and bread and flour rationed for a while in that July. Clothes remained a problem, for the royal family as for everyone else, and were to remain rationed for another three years, but despite the difficulties, people everywhere had had enough of drabness and stringency. The young people in particular, those who had grown up during the war years, had missed almost all the amusements that were their due, and they were determined to make up for lost time. There could be little lavishness on the prewar scale; the clock could never be turned back for any side of life, social or otherwise, but entertainment and social life of a limited sort quickly got under way once more. Elizabeth was in much demand on the London scene, and there were photographs of her in the glossy magazines dining out at 'in' places like the Bagatelle, or enjoying big occasions such as the Commando Ball of June 1946. Princess Anne, who considers it an excellent thing that her father had the opportunity to 'get around' unimpeded as a young man, is probably correct in her shrewd surmise that, within limits, her mother did so as well, and to a greater extent than she is going to admit to a liberty-conscious daughter!

Certainly the King and Queen encouraged Elizabeth to enjoy herself in young society, and they were very conscious of the deprivations induced by war conditions. Possibly they also thought it a good idea that she should meet as large a cross-section of personable young men as possible. A contemporary writer commented that the name 'Philip' was cropping up increasingly often in the future Queen's conversation, and since it still does today, the report was likely to be true. The press noted that Prince Philip of Greece was squiring the Princess on social occasions. He was with her at the reception at the Savoy when she was bridesmaid at her lady-in-waiting's wedding, and they went to many of the same parties. Philip was there with the royal family when both Princesses were bridesmaids at the marriage of Lord Louis Mountbatten's daughter in Romsey Abbey, and one paper headlined the 'significance' of his helping Lilibet on with her coat! The rumours were beginning to fly, and although the Palace categorically denied any romance, to the family it must have been very clear that Lilibet was in love.

Apart from all the complex considerations at a national and state level that have to be taken into account when a royal marriage is contemplated, and particularly one involving the Heiress Presumptive, the King also had to deal with his personal feelings as a father. They were much the same as those experienced by most men in this situation. Lilibet was only twenty, to her parents still a mere child, and owing to her special circumstances had led a more than ordinarily sheltered life. Did she really know her own mind? How could she be sure Philip was the right one when she had met so few other eligible young men? Just at a time when she was beginning to savour some of the enjoyments that are the right of youth, did she really want to settle down and add the responsibilities of marriage to a life that was bound to become rapidly and increasingly onerous? This was the kind of question that worried the King through that spring and early summer of 1946, and perhaps there was tucked away unacknowledged at the bottom of the list the fear of disturbing the family circle and home life that were the source of his personal happiness.

Whatever their private thoughts may have been, the two most concerned did not apparently get round to discussing marriage until Philip was invited to Scotland that year to spend a month of late summer with the family at Balmoral. Even then, when an evening paper suggested an engagement was imminent, the King's private secretary could put out a perfectly truthful disclaimer. Philip and Elizabeth were not engaged yet, or at least not officially. The King and Queen, however, had available a course of action that many parents in a similar situation would like to take. Within a short while they were due to leave for South Africa, on an official tour that would last until the following May, and Elizabeth was to go with them. This was an interval welcomed alike by the family, as an opportune separation during which Lilibet and Philip could make quite sure of their feelings, and by the Government as a respite for both the country and the Dominions to discuss the idea and get used to the possibility of a marriage.

There was nothing personal in this caution. With the exception of some of the 'older guard' at Court who found his breezy personality disturbing to say the least, all who knew Philip liked him, and there could be nothing but praise for his naval and war service records and respect for his principles and character. Nor could the idea of this marriage have come as a complete surprise to the royal family. As far back as 1941 Philip's aunt, Princess Nicholas, had implied to Sir Henry Channon that her nephew was serving in the British Navy as a prelude to becoming the British Prince Consort. That was, of course, pure and (at the time) incorrect surmise, arising from the manner in which most relations think and talk. ('He is eligible, he is the sort of person she might marry . . .'; therefore it is a *fait accompli*, QED!) But as Prince Philip also points out, his name was sure to have been on the list, so to speak, because the number of 'possibles' was not very extensive. Anyway, King George of Greece had already put in a word on Philip's behalf as a suitor, although the notion had received small encouragement on account of Elizabeth's youth.

That was the rub. No doubt the King and Queen had discussed and pondered the matter many times, but Lilibet was too young and, like numerous parents of young daughters, they shelved any thought of marriage as an idea related only to some vague moment in the future, a formless consideration that was difficult to accept as a possible fact.

Politically, on both home and foreign fronts, Philip was a bit of a problem. His naturalization was still held up although, as an aspirant to British citizenship, he had already obtained the Greek King's assent to his renouncing any place in the succession to the Greek throne. But with Archbishop Damaskinos acting as regent in the troubled Greek situation and because there was no certainty that the King would be able to return, the matter could be taken in two ways: either as a sign of British support for the Greek royalists, an implication not entirely acceptable to the British Government; or conversely as an unfortunate indication that Prince Philip was abandoning a sinking ship!

It seemed prudent to let things slide until after the plebiscite in Greece, held early in 1946. This resulted in the Greek King's regaining his throne in the following autumn. But then another question arose. Since Prince Philip was in direct succession, might it not harm the monarchist cause if he renounced his Greek nationality just at that time?

It was all sorted out eventually, and then only the choice of an appropriate title remained. The suggested 'His Royal Highness Prince Philip' was a right and privilege the King was happy to grant, but Philip declined the honour – a decision that impressed his future father-in-law. Once he was a British subject he would prefer to be known simply as 'Lieutenant Philip . . . RN', with the surname of Mountbatten decided on later after some thought. This arrangement, once the *London Gazette* of 18 March 1947 had carried the announcement, was to dispose of any Government disquiet concerning a marriage between Princess Elizabeth, as Heiress Presumptive, and one who was closely connected with the varying and uncertain fortunes of the royal Greek regime.

In the meantime none of this made life any easier for Philip. He had come back to England in *Whelp*, with some of the prisoners-of-war from South-East Asia aboard, and on arrival at Portsmouth, as second-in-command, he was put in charge of his ship's recommission. During the two months spent on the job Philip, like Elizabeth, had an opportunity, if with considerably more scope, to catch up on some of the gaieties denied in his case by a war service that had begun when he was eighteen. His combination of good looks, attractive personality and royal status ensured Philip the maximum of social dates. He dined, danced, played cricket, mixed in at the local pub, enjoyed it all and was fairly relentlessly pursued.

After the weeks at Balmoral a new job as instructor found him at Cosham, and from there his MG sports car was frequently headed at some speed for London, and usually for Buckingham Palace – where an unobtrusive entry was sometimes made through the tradesmen's entrance. Sometimes, when it headed out again, Elizabeth was in the passenger seat.

It was the month's leave at Balmoral that gave them the first real opportunity of being together for any length of time. Then there were the lunches and visits to the Palace, and Philip joined the family at Sandringham for Christmas. At last it was possible to get to know each other within the context of their new relationship.

Those were good times, but even then it was not all plain sailing, particularly for Philip.

From the purely personal angle falling in love with a princess, even with one who is the Heiress Presumptive, is no different from falling in love with anyone else. The feelings are the same, though some of the implications are more thought-provoking than usual, and could be almost terrifying viewed in the abstract. And the setting, right from the start, is considerably more public.

It seems that, with Philip anyway, the early liking and companionship did not deepen into anything much more until around the spring of 1946, but specific dates are impossible to name and when it happened, it happened.

ELIZABETH AND PHILIP

By the time of Philip's stay at Balmoral marriage appeared such an obvious course that it would have been difficult for them to remember when things were not on that basis. But even so there must have been a great deal of straight thinking and most serious consideration before Philip came to that point, and most of it for the sake of Elizabeth's ultimate good and happiness. Despite the significance of the royal heritage to a man of some natural ambition, the implications for a keen, serving naval officer with an innate love of personal freedom of speech and action and a built-in distaste for publicity required thought enough. It was to be hoped that the day on which his wife would become Her Majesty Queen Elizabeth II was still far in the future, but even so it was so weighty a matter, in many ways so difficult to visualize, that maybe Philip thought it best to defer most of the deliberations to that far-distant date as well. But if he had not had the self-knowledge to feel sure that as husband of the Queen he could make a worthwhile contribution, if there had not been the confidence to believe he could ease the immense load Elizabeth would have to carry, Philip's acute awareness of the enormous responsibilities involved would have overpowered any personal feelings.

The guess is that it was much simpler for Elizabeth. As her father's daughter and with her own character and training she, too, would never let private emotion take precedence over what she saw to be her duty, but when it was indisputably clear to her, and had been for some time, that Philip was the right and only man on both counts, then perhaps her only problem was to convince the King and Queen that she knew her own mind.

On this point the African tour could only be a help. On return everyone must surely realize that a separation of four months had only intensified their regard for each other. Apart from this consideration Elizabeth knew it would give her father much happiness to have all his family with him on a tour to which he had been looking forward for a year or more and one which he felt was of particular importance for strengthening Commonwealth ties, and for giving him further opportunity to meet more people and know more of the lands within his rule. Politically it was also a good idea that Princess Elizabeth should go. As a Dominion South Africa was implicated in any marriage she might make, and it was diplomatic that many people should have the chance to see and meet the Princess for themselves. Possibly there would also be some who would remember Prince Philip of Greece from the time when his ship put in at Cape Town during the war.

ROMANCE AND ENGAGEMENT

It was not easy to leave Philip, particularly at a time when his natural impatience at the hold-up in both his engagement and the naturalization that was one of its prerequisites was being exacerbated by a growing public interest in his personal affairs. But maybe Elizabeth's inherent common sense persuaded her it was for the best, and just before her wedding she was to write to her mother to say that the long wait had been no bad thing.

The royal family boarded HMS *Vanguard* on 1 February and for the next three weeks they were able to relax, reading, playing games, dancing, competing on a rifle range (where Elizabeth proved she had inherited her father's marksmanship); and for the Princesses there was the hilarious ritual of crossing the line – although they were spared the customary ducking.

They landed at Cape Town on 17 February to an exuberant welcome from the massed crowds, and to the start of a strenuous programme that included thousands of miles of travelling by train, car and aeroplane.

They set off, after the King had performed the most important ceremony, the opening of the Union Parliament, across the lovely lands of the Cape to East London, where Elizabeth opened the graving-dock that bears her name. The next part of their itinerary took them north to what was then the Rhodesias, with a stop-off *en route* at the Kimberley diamond mines, and east again through the Orange Free State, Basutoland (now Lesotho), and so to Natal. And it was while enjoying a well-earned rest, staying at the hostel in Natal's National Park, that Elizabeth learned the welcome news that Prince Philip of Greece had become Lieutenant Philip Mountbatten, RN, an acknowledged citizen of Britain.

Other news from Britain had not been so good. The royal voyage and tour had coincided with one of the worst winters ever, with endless frost and blizzards, and fuel shortages resulting in real hardship. The King was so worried at being absent at such a time that he wished to interrupt the tour and fly home, but was persuaded that South Africa took priority.

Elizabeth celebrated her twenty-first birthday on the return to Cape Town. The day was declared a public holiday throughout the Dominion, the Princess reviewed a parade of the South African Army, and before the evening's giant display of fireworks and the glittering State Ball at Government House that followed, she broadcast a message to her father's peoples. It was simple, short and to the point. It was also transparently sincere, and the pledge made when the Queen was twenty-one is being faithfully implemented today. '. . . I declare before you all,' she said, 'that my whole life, whether it be long or short, shall be devoted to your service . . .' And that is the way it still is.

They said goodbye to South Africa three days later and set sail for home. The King was content. Despite the inevitable fatigue there had been much to enjoy and much of interest, and he felt relaxed, happy at the friendliness encountered and able to return to work refreshed, with a mission well completed.

Elizabeth was content too. She was returning to the man she loved, a state of mind written clearly on her face for all to see as they landed. But still there was no official announcement of an engagement.

The Princess was now of age, but that made no difference to the fact that her engagement and intended marriage remained subjects of family, political and Dominion consideration. As for the British public, there had been rumours enough even before the South African tour, and possibly even Philip's sense of humour had been a little over-taxed when a national paper ran the equivalent of a modern opinion poll on the desirability of the whole affair. The findings were: forty per cent against his marrying Elizabeth at all; five per cent for its not being politically opposed provided she renounced her claim to the throne; and a consoling fifty-five per cent in favour, so long as the two of them were in love. It must have been difficult not to take exception to a mounting public intrusion into what the principals could scarcely help considering their own personal concern.

During the weeks while Elizabeth was away Philip was doing his best to carry on normally with his career in spite of all the temper-fraying publicity. He must have been thinking that once the naturalization was through there would be no time lost before making the engagement announcement, but still nothing happened.

It is very probable that much of the delay was a result of the state of the country at that time. Since the end of the war life, instead of getting easier, had become increasingly geared to austerity and utility. War-time rationing and controls remained and were in some instances increased, and on top of a disastrous winter and the devastating floods that followed, direct and indirect taxes were spiralling and there were drastic cuts in imports of such day-to-day necessities as fuel and newsprint. The new Supplies and Services Bill did not become law until August that year, but was already threatening further cuts in food and luxuries, and in investment both private and public. The clauses giving power of direction in certain industries as to where a man could work and at what were causing the severest disquiet, with Mr Churchill in Opposition thundering about '. . . a blank cheque for totalitarian government'.

The King had become increasingly anxious about the economic position, and he may have felt it was not a propitious moment to make an announcement about something that was in itself controversial. Whatever the reasons for the previous delay, on 9 July 1947 there was an addition to the Court Circular, and all the world knew what it had been suspecting for some time – that the King and Queen gladly gave their consent to the betrothal of their beloved daughter, the Princess Elizabeth, to Lieutenant Philip Mountbatten, RN.

On the evening before, during a pre-announcement family dinner party at the Palace, after the King had made a short speech Philip produced the ring and slipped it on Elizabeth's finger. He had wanted to make it a symbol of special significance in his own family, and the design, chosen by Elizabeth, was made up in diamonds taken from a ring that Philip's father had given to his mother many years before. At his request his mother Princess Alice had brought it to England in time to be re-set, and she was there to see her son and future daughter-in-law make their first promise to each other.

Once the engagement was an established fact public opinion swung in Philip's favour and the people took him to their hearts, to the position that Elizabeth already held. They forgot the former rumblings about the Princess's making an 'alien' marriage, recalled that his mother was British, that the Danish royal house had produced Queen Alexandra, and that his cousin Marina, a Greek princess, was already established as a well-loved member of the royal family.

On the day of the announcement enormous crowds milled about in front of the Palace singing 'All the Nice Girls Love a Sailor', and by evening were getting a number of 'first' appearances of the engaged couple in response to their insistent demands. That afternoon there was a Palace garden party where Philip and Elizabeth, showered with congratulations and good wishes, had a good foretaste of the days to come.

It was a foregone conclusion that every known and surmised fact about Princess Elizabeth would be refurbished to fill the world news sheets, but it astonished Philip to find just how many details were unearthed concerning his way of life, family history, likes and dislikes, all in meticulous detail if not all strictly accurate, until he felt like an inmate of the zoo. Surprisingly even the Admiralty co-operated with public demand and press photographs appeared of Lieutenant Mountbatten's modest quarters at Cosham, iron bedstead, chest-of-drawers, family pictures and all.

Part of an immediate fourteen days' leave was spent with the royal family at Holyrood House. No need now for tactful secrecy or an impossible front of assumed lack of interest, and whether the attractive young pair were dancing together at a Youth and Services Ball held at the Edinburgh Assembly Rooms or at one of the several regimental balls they attended, whether it was a private engagement or whether Philip was with the Princess on an official occasion such as when she received the freedom of Edinburgh, they were the cynosure of universal attention that was approving, admiring and delighted. Nowadays it may be a cliché to say 'all the world loves a lover', but that is how it was for most people, and possibly still is, and the obvious happiness, good looks, gaiety and charm of Elizabeth and Philip provided an enchanting alternative to the gloomy state of the economy and the drabness of life in general.

Philip began his own public life modestly enough by unveiling a war memorial at Cosham. He was continuing normal service with the Navy and was determined to persist with his career, but even so life was changing fast. With characteristic thoroughness he set out to learn all the rules and regulations governing Court procedure and Palace formalities, including those he was to bend or give a dusting to in the years to come.

With his innate good manners combined with a friendly and gregarious nature it was not difficult to master the essentials still outstanding. But possibly only Elizabeth could appreciate how hard it was for him even to think of always being discreet, of curbing some of his high spirits and damping down the loud infectious laugh, to contemplate being circumspect where it was natural for him to be outspoken. And of course, although time has brought about a little of this, nothing and nobody could ever stop Philip from remaining basically his candid self – and no doubt Elizabeth had already realized this and, like a great number of people today, thanked heaven for it.

Philip must have had occasional moments of doubt and anxiety about the formidable public and state side of his future life, and certainly for one so unadapted to royal conventions necessities like his own detective, forced on him by increasing public interest, would be irritants. He would have been fully aware that some sections of the Court were still apprehensive about the

Foreign visitors and foreign travel take them away from home

President Nixon in animated conversation with the Queen and
Prince Philip when he arrived for lunch.

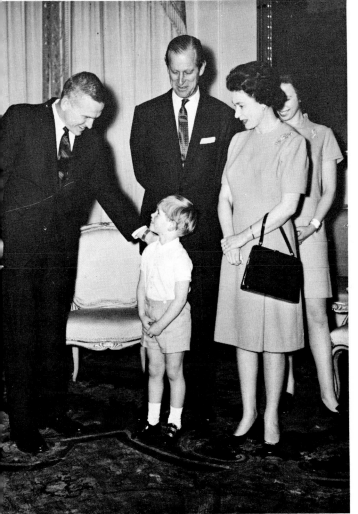

Top left In Ethiopia, Emperor Haile Selassie shows his visitors the Tississah Falls

Above The Queen and Prince Philip negotiate an awkward staircase at the ancient palace of Gondar (Ethiopia)

The American astronaut, Frank Borman, struck up a great friendship with Prince Edward when he visited Buckingham Palace

Opposite page They also have to find time in their official calendar for travelling abroad. One of their early state visits was to France where they inspected a guard of honour at the Arc de Triomphe (*above*)

Another important part of the Royal Family's life is the entertaining of foreign visitors. *Below* President Eisenhower waves a greeting to the crowds as he arrives on a visit at Balmoral in 1959

Prince Philip at the
Soukh in Marrakesh
stops to watch two
Moroccan snake
charmers

Driving in an old fashioned carriage on the way to visit one of Prince Philip's sisters at
Salem castle, his old school, which was later evacuated to Gordonstoun

After a six-week visit to Canada, all the family are waiting to meet the Queen and Prince Philip at the airport

Prince Philip exchanging a few private words with the Queen at a state banquet in Brussels

Left One of the home comforts accompanying the Queen and Prince Philip on a visit to Chile is a London policeman

Right The Queen and Prince Philip arriving by boat at an evening party in Norway

Opposite above Mingling with the crowds without a barrier of troops or policemen is a new and much enjoyed departure for the royal family. The Queen, Prince Philip and their two eldest children are threading their way among the crowd at Picton in New Zealand

Opposite below At the Parthenon in Athens

Well insulated against the biting cold, Prince Philip, the Queen and Princess Anne
walking down the main street of Tuktyaktuk in Arctic Canada

role, obviously far from static, that the future Queen's husband might be going to play, and possibly gained inward amusement from occasionally stepping up their fears. But then as now, it was thought for Elizabeth that was Philip's chief concern.

By the end of July the King had formally approved the marriage at a meeting of the Privy Council, and the date was fixed for 20 November. This announcement promptly sparked off another controversy in both Government and public over the style of the ceremony, one faction arguing that at a time of economic crisis only a relatively austere ceremony could be entertained, the other considering it high time Britain had some colourful jollification to relieve the overall monotony, and what better moment than this?

Once more it all died down and the weeks began to fly. Elizabeth, with Philip there to support her when he could get leave, was in constant demand for functions, and if the public arrangements for the wedding were out of their hands, she had plenty of personal matters to see to and was no doubt thankful that Margaret was by then a working member of the royal team.

Philip, who was baptized into the Greek Orthodox Church, had his religious position regularized by admission into the Church of England. The seemingly insoluble problem of a guest list, of world-wide import but limited by precedence and the size of Westminster Abbey, was eventually unravelled to the general satisfaction of all except those who felt they should have been included, and the invitations were sent out. Presents, literally thousands of them and all soon to be on show in the cause of charity at St James's Palace, began rolling in. The Treasury began taking official interest, at import regulation level, in the spun silk used for the bridal gown, but happily it turned out to be of British origin. On top of all the items of protocol and administration that came within their province, the executive staff at the Palace spent much of their days, and possibly some of their nights, dealing with suggestions, requests, and criticisms which arrived by the truck-load.

Arrangements, later acknowledged to be somewhat inadequate, although unavoidably so, were made for coverage of the wedding ceremony by the British and Dominion press, and the King's veto on filming and televising was amended. At last the preparations were all but complete, and on dates separated by eight days of seniority, the King gave Elizabeth and Philip the honour of the oldest order of chivalry, the Most Noble Order of the Garter.

E

ELIZABETH AND PHILIP

The evening of 19 November arrived, when the King and Queen were trying to disguise from Elizabeth their natural sadness at losing her, and Philip was participating in his last party as a bachelor. He had just been authorized by the King's personal prerogative to take the prefix 'His Royal Highness' (although he was not, officially, a British royal prince until 1957), and created Baron Greenwich (for England), Earl of Merioneth (for Wales), and Duke of Edinburgh (for Scotland).

Marriage, children, and tragedy

IT was a cold, grey day on 20 November 1947, with only the glimpse of a wintry sun to relieve it, but the weather was no deterrent to the immense crowds that since the previous night had been packing themselves on to the pavements between Buckingham Palace and Westminster Abbey, and filling Trafalgar Square to capacity so that Lord Nelson stood aloft, rising from a sea of faces.

The people were out to be with Elizabeth and Philip on their great day, their wedding day, out to have as many glimpses as they could of the young pair whose romance had caught the imagination of the world, and to wish them in all sincerity good luck and God's blessing. They were there to greet the King and Queen and demonstrate yet again what so many foreigners find difficult to understand, that loyalty and affection in which the majority of the British hold the Crown and the royal family. They were out to take their fill of an occasion of colour and pageantry and goodwill, an opportunity to sweep some of the drab austerities of the post-war world out of sight under the red carpets. And they were not disappointed.

The troops helping the police to line the route were wearing the only-too familiar khaki, but the Household Brigade were back in the almost forgotten glories of full-dress uniform. Out from the moth-balled storage of the past eight years came the black bearskins and burnished chin-straps, the red-striped blue trousers and blue tunics with the different button-groupings of the five regiments of Foot Guards. When the various mounted escorts of Household Cavalry clattered by, on roads specially sanded for the benefit of all the processional horses, the public had a nostalgic eyeful of the blue tunics and red-plumed helmets of the Royal Horse Guards, the red tunics and white plumes of the Life Guards, the gleaming breastplates and drawn swords and boots polished to match the shine on the coats of their black chargers. They made a fitting setting for the splendid equipages they accompanied.

There was the carriage bearing Her Majesty the Queen and seventeen-year-old Princess Margaret, the chief bridesmaid; there was the one carrying Queen Mary, gracious, dignified, seated still straight as a ram-rod for all her eighty years; and after many more, there at last, leaving the Palace at precisely sixteen minutes past eleven o'clock, was the Glass Coach, drawn by a pair of Windsor greys, and driven by the head coachman resplendent in the scarlet and gold of semi-state livery.

The Glass Coach gets its name from the size of the windows and so only those at the very back of the crowds were thwarted in their desire to have a good view of the occupants. There was the King in the gold-braided uniform of Admiral of the Fleet, his expression the same mixture of pride and concern, happiness and sadness worn by so many fathers on such occasions, and there beside him was Elizabeth. She looked very lovely in her richly embroidered but simply cut wedding dress, pearls round her throat, a small diadem holding the veil in place over her brown hair and, according to royal custom, away from her face. She looked calm, unmistakably happy – radiant is the now out-dated expression – enchantingly natural, and very young.

Inside the Abbey the guests were waiting, members of the British royal family together with one of the century's largest gatherings of foreign kings, queens and princes, whether reigning or exiled; distinguished leaders of the Commonwealth, church dignitaries, leading members of His Majesty's Government and Opposition, peers, peeresses, and the other lucky but less exalted two thousand who were privileged to be present. The bridegroom was waiting with his best man, seated in his appointed place beside the steps of the sacrarium. The uniform of a first lieutenant was decorated with war and service medals and the newly presented eight-pointed star of the Garter, and he carried the sword that had belonged to his grandfather, Prince Louis of Battenberg. He sat waiting, judging the approach of his bride by the intensifying clamour of cheering that not even the seven-hundred-year-old walls of the Abbey could entirely deaden.

They were married by special licence by the Archbishop of Canterbury, who was assisted by the Dean of Westminster. Though the setting was splendid and the music and singing beautiful beyond measure, the simple form of service was the same as that used at any Anglican church wedding in the land. And when it came to the familiar vows, bride and groom made their pledges with such sincerity and conviction that the King's last lingering doubts vanished. He knew for sure that 'everything was all right'.

The register was signed in the presence of the King and Queen, Queen Mary, Princess Alice, Princess Margaret, Princess Marina and fourteen others. Then, while the great Abbey organ pealed and the clamour of the bells heralded their coming, the Duke of Edinburgh and his bride, Princess Elizabeth the Duchess of Edinburgh, processed slowly together down the length of the big church and out into the acclamation of the hundreds of thousands awaiting them.

For the honeymoon, Lord Louis Mountbatten had lent them Broadlands, his lovely home near Romsey, which Philip had come to know well as a schoolboy, and where until marriage he had had his own room.

There and in the grounds, kept secluded behind clipped yew hedges, these two should surely have been able to find, alone together, the peace that was their due. But the attentions of the press, and of the sightseers who poured into the district to gather outside the gates and around the estate boundaries, drove Philip and Elizabeth north to Scotland, where the people pride themselves on minding their manners and, within reason, leaving the royal family alone.

They went to Birkhall, the sequestered Georgian house on Deeside, close by Balmoral, which is today one of the Queen Mother's favourite homes. Originally it was bought for Edward VII when he was Prince of Wales, and when it proved too small Abergeldie Castle was leased for his use. But the gay Edward, like the next king of his name, found Scotland too remote for his tastes.

Elizabeth's father loved Birkhall from boyhood days, and his daughter would remember the mounting excitement with which she and Margaret looked forward to the annual holiday in the same house in the years before the accession, and wonder at how little she had known at the time of her parent's anxieties clouding the last holiday they had at Birkhall together in the fateful August of 1936. It was during those weeks when the royal family were trying to accept the fact, at that time unknown to the British public, that the King, Edward VIII, had fallen deeply in love with someone who could never share his throne, a time when the Duke of York, as next in line, had to contemplate the dreaded reality of his being called on to be King himself.

But there were no shadows to mar Philip's and Elizabeth's happiness together at Birkhall, in the short time they had before re-emerging into the public eye.

They came south to Windsor in time for the King's birthday on 14 December and then moved into temporary quarters in Buckingham Palace. Clarence House, their London home, was not yet ready for occupation and

Sunningdale Manor, near Ascot, the proposed country refuge, had been burned down.

This arrangement was obviously not ideal, no young married couple really wants to live with the family however good the relationship, but even if, through circumstances outside anybody's control, they could not yet do much about making a home, it was, nevertheless, a time when they could start building up their working partnership. Philip was still very much in the Navy and occupied with his service career, but a successful combination of naval duties with those connected with his wife's and his own public life was helped along by a temporary appointment to the Naval Operations Division. It was not perhaps an over-exciting job for one who likes an active life, but it was convenient for its location in Whitehall and its nine-to-five working hours.

He could get time off for those enjoyable engagements that involved them both. Sometimes he was able to go along in a purely supporting role, and Elizabeth found the most onerous functions lightened and made easy by a delightful and reliable companion, whose spontaneous remarks relieved the stiffest formality, who was always on the look-out to make things easier for her, and was capable of making her laugh at the most nerve-racking moments.

Now and again it was the Princess who did the sustaining, when, for example, she sat in one of the Secretaries' boxes near the throne to watch her husband take his seat in the House of Lords, or when they were together in the Guildhall for Prince Philip to receive the freedom of London, and again when he accepted the same honour at Greenwich.

As the weeks passed there were growing demands for Philip to open an exhibition, present a cup or speak at an all-male dinner. The speeches were proving a success, and the scope was endless for one who was certainly no cypher, who could speak 'off the cuff' when necessary, and had individualistic, worthwhile, often controversial views to offer, all seasoned with pleasing self-mockery and an entertaining wit. So sometimes, while Elizabeth was returning from an engagement of her own (inspecting troops about to leave for overseas, attending a sitting of the South-East London Juvenile Court, or opening the central shopping square at re-built Coventry), Philip would be dashing back from Whitehall to change for one of his evening commitments. By the time the Admiralty job had come to an end and Philip was attending a course at the Staff College in Greenwich, the outside pressures were mounting sharply, the division of labour was becoming well established and the pattern of the public side of their life had started to emerge.

On 26 April 1948 the King and Queen celebrated their silver wedding, a day of personal thanksgiving for the twenty-five years of happiness they had found together and of re-dedication to their life of service, also celebrated on a more public level by an appreciative nation. No doubt to Philip and Elizabeth, by then married for five months, it was a happy and moving anniversary – and one quite impossible to visualize in their own far-off future.

In May Philip and Elizabeth crossed the Channel for a semi-state visit to Paris as a first, moderately gentle introduction to future foreign commitments.

From the point of view of the 'entente', first made particularly 'cordiale' by Elizabeth's great-grandfather Edward VII and worn a little thin by the happenings of the Second World War, the enterprise was a big success. They played the public role well, and the welcome became almost overwhelming. The Princess opened an exhibition depicting the British way of life, they called on the President, visited Versailles, laid a wreath on the tomb of the Unknown Soldier, attended a reception given by the Municipal Council, and a gala performance at the Opera House, and Prince Philip was honoured with the presentation of the *Croix de Guerre* by Monsieur Auriol. Everywhere they were applauded and acclaimed and it was all very heartwarming, but if Philip had any ideas that the semi-official status of the visit might allow them to go off so that he could show his young wife, on her first visit to the Continent, round a lovely city that he knows well, the swarming crowds and legions of photographers soon made him realize his mistake. Maybe that was the moment it fully dawned on him that the privacy Elizabeth had never known was now a thing of the past for him also.

When they arrived home it must, moreover, have been puzzling and hurtful to find that the innocuous pastimes of their Sunday in France – after church a visit to the races at Longchamps with the President and his wife, dining together in the evening at a fashionable restaurant with a view across the Seine to the lovely, illuminated outline of Notre Dame – had outraged a section of the strict Sabbatarians who were voicing their disapproval in the national press. Maybe that too was a pointer to what all members of the royal family come to accept, that it is almost impossible to please everyone, all the time.

Windlesham Moor, a house in Surrey, had been leased early in the year and

Philip and Elizabeth had been using it at weekends, but by the autumn the move from the Palace to this temporary home was complete. To their joy Elizabeth was having a baby, but there was a cloud lying over their happiness. The King was ill, and although this was not public knowledge until late autumn, the Navy agreed to put Philip on half-pay when his course at Greenwich ended in September, enabling him to shoulder more royal responsibilities without actually leaving the service.

In the spring of 1948 it had seemed as though the King had at last recovered from the strains of the war, but soon bouts of cramp, which he ignored, developed into continual pain and discomfort in his feet, and when he at last consulted his doctor at the end of October, the report was an alarming one. With a characteristic sense of duty added to the determination not to alarm Elizabeth just when her baby was almost due, the King continued with his commitments, even the most exacting, up to and after 12 November when specialists confirmed that he was suffering from hardening of the arteries, with a real danger of gangrene developing and subsequent amputation of his leg.

No public announcement about the King's condition was made until 16 November, after he had reluctantly agreed to the postponement of a proposed tour of Australia and New Zealand in the following spring, two days after Princess Elizabeth had had a son.

Charles Philip Arthur George was born at Buckingham Palace at fourteen minutes past nine on the evening of 14 November, the first male in direct line of succession for nearly sixty years and, like the majority of babies, the pride and joy of his young parents.

Yet again the crowds were out in front of the Palace, cheering, chanting 'For He's a Jolly Good Fellow', mobbing Queen Mary's car to give her affectionate greetings on becoming a great-grandmother, and continuing their noisy celebrations until a request was circulated among the throng, asking them to go home so that everyone could get some sleep.

For a week the fountains in Trafalgar Square spouted water 'blue for a boy', and five days before his grandson's birth the King had overruled edicts that could have precluded the baby from the right to a princely title, by issuing letters patent under the Great Seal ensuring this and all future children of the Duke and Duchess of Edinburgh the designation of Prince or Princess. By this means Charles Philip Arthur George, who might have had only the customary courtesy use of his father's second title, the Earl of Merioneth, could rightfully become known to the world at large as His Royal Highness Prince Charles of Edinburgh. At home the baby Charles was bringing Philip and Elizabeth all the new delights and responsibilities and all the adjustments required by their new role, just as they are experienced by most parents with their first-born.

In the New Year of 1949 the King's health improved sufficiently for him to undertake a few audiences and an investiture, but it was soon apparent that an operation was imperative if he was not to remain a complete invalid. A complicated lumbar sympathectomy was carried out on 12 March, but this time there were no noisy celebrations from the waiting crowds when the news came, 'He's all right,' but only a deep feeling of thankfulness, shared throughout the country and world.

Despite a good recovery, from then on the King had to slow down the tempo of his life to some extent and that summer was a very full one for Philip and Elizabeth, for they had even more public functions, the shared fun and delight of their small son's big adventure of growing up, and the move, at last, into Clarence House in early July.

Austerity was still very much the order of the day and it was not the easiest of moments to set up house, but it was wonderful to have the ordering of their own ideas and tastes under the roof of their very own home. Elizabeth's upbringing would scarcely have included housework, but she has always been domestically minded and even in the vast anachronism of Buckingham Palace likes to see for herself that guest rooms are 'just so'. In that first home she could give full rein to her practical mind, discussing with Philip and their workmen such mundane problems as the best siting of electrical points, while her husband, no lover of gimmicks for their own sake but enthusiastic about time-saving modernizations, was equally involved.

Towards the end of the summer the King was so much better that it was possible for Philip to resume his career, and in October he flew out to take up an appointment as first lieutenant in HMS *Chequers*, based on Malta and the leader of the First Mediterranean Fleet. Early in November Elizabeth went out to join him.

Lord Louis Mountbatten loaned them his house, the Villa Guardamangia on the outskirts of Valetta, with the sun-drenched town and harbour laid out for their delight below the stone-worked balustrade of the balcony. Within their grasp now was the only short interlude in their life together to date when they have been, almost, free.

ELIZABETH AND PHILIP

Inevitably there was always a detective around, there were a very few formal occasions and once or twice Elizabeth felt she should pay a visit to some local institution. Otherwise, just like everyone else, she was free to go out to the shops to buy food for that evening's impromptu party; to go to the hairdresser like any of the other service wives, or to join them to chat and laugh on the polo field where Philip, with more enthusiasm than skill, was making his first essays at the game. There were picnics and boating parties and all the lighthearted amusements of a crowd of young people out to enjoy themselves in a sunny climate, and Philip and Elizabeth made the most of every carefree minute.

When *Chequers* was detailed for patrol in the Red Sea after Christmas, with the Mediterranean Fleet's spring cruise to follow, Elizabeth went home to her small son and her public duties. She was able to rejoin Philip in Malta again for a while in April 1950, until *Chequers* sailed for Alexandria and Elizabeth returned to England to await the birth of their second child.

Philip came home on leave in that July and was there for a double celebration, for the birth of his daughter, Anne Elizabeth Alice Louise, on 15 August, and for his own promotion, gazetted lieutenant-commander with a ship of his own, the frigate *Magpie*.

He joined his ship in September, and after a return to London in October for the baby's christening, settled down to a job after his own heart – turning *Magpie* into what she soon became, 'cock ship' of the squadron in everything from smartness and efficiency to being principal winner in the annual regatta. But with all this activity the royal commitments were not forgotten; wherever *Magpie* put in her commander acted most successfully as an unofficial ambassador of Whitehall, and in November that year the Duke flew to Gibraltar to represent the King at the official opening of the Legislative Assembly. Later in the month Elizabeth again came out to Malta and they sailed for a semi-official visit to Greece.

There was no suitable accommodation for the commander's wife on board *Magpie* and Elizabeth sailed in the dispatch vessel *Surprise*, but it was a delightful voyage westwards across the Ionian Sea and through the Gulf of Corinth into the narrow, sheer-sided slip of the Corinth Canal, with Elizabeth adding to the general gaiety by helping to concoct the lighthearted signals exchanged between the ships.

Athens was *en fête* for their arrival, but despite the formalities there was opportunity for Philip to show Elizabeth round and meet many of his innumerable relations, and for informal excursions along the entrancing Greek coastline. It was all part of the natural wish of two young people to be together as much as possible, even if it did mean leaving two babies occasionally in the care of devoted and experienced nannies, and in the overall loving charge of the King and Queen, and of their Strathmore grandparents. Yet there were people to criticize the Princess for doing just that.

Indeed, by the following April Philip and Elizabeth were again under fire, this time from the Free Church of Scotland for 'going out of their way to visit the Vatican and do obeisance to the head of the Roman Catholic hierarchy' – one way of describing a short but very worthwhile audience with the Pope, that erudite diplomat Pius XII.

At home again, Elizabeth was successfully combining the life of a conscientious and loving mother of two lively children and chatelaine of Clarence House with an almost incessant round of public duties. Philip was back to join with her in the ceremonial opening of the Festival of Britain in May. By July he was back for good, on indefinite leave that marked the end of any further active service with the Navy.

On 3 May 1951 the King had stood on the steps of St Paul's Cathedral to declare open the nationwide festival, designed to demonstrate to the world Britain's recovery from the war. Shortly afterwards he was to face entertaining a foreign Head of State, was looking forward to going to Ireland with the Queen, and was overjoyed that the postponed Australasian tour was to go forward in the spring of 1952. But there was public comment on the King's drawn appearance, and his family's anxiety was deepening. On 24 May, although feeling unwell, he insisted on going in state to install the Duke of Gloucester as Great Master of the Order of the Bath. Influenza developed with a worryingly slow recovery, and on 8 September an X-ray confirmed the doctors' suspicions. The King had lung cancer but, as far as is known, he never realized the fact, and his family concealed their knowledge with loving concern and the same courage the King himself displayed in facing an operation to remove one lung.

The operation proved more dangerous even than anticipated, but gradually some of the King's strength returned and by the middle of October he was writing to Queen Mary: '... at last I am feeling a little better ...' In the meantime he was happy and proud to know how well Philip and Elizabeth were carrying out their added responsibilities.

Philip had enjoyed his twelve years in the Navy, the command of his own ship *Magpie* had meant the attainment of one of his great ambitions and his future prospects were very bright. It must have caused him great distress to leave the service, and *Magpie* and her crew in particular, but with his marriage he had accepted that one day this must happen, and Philip has never been one to long for the unattainable. If this complete break in his life had come sooner than hoped, then that was just unfortunate. The King needed him, his place was with Elizabeth to give the strength and support he had promised her, and it was good to be with wife and children, living in his own home. Life and work had moved into new but not unknown fields and it was time to get on with the job. Even if neither Philip nor anyone else was quite sure what that might turn out to be in the end, there were pointers.

In 1949 when Prince Philip became president of the National Playing Fields Association he had made very clear his interest in youth and the problems of youth. From his first speech and subsequent activities it also became clear that here was someone who would never be content just to lend his name to any enterprise he undertook. Shades of Gordonstoun and the 'two-hundred-per-center' character were apparent, and as his undertakings grew in variety and number, a lot of people had to start sitting up and taking notice. After Philip was elected president of the Association for the Advancement of Science for 1951–2, and in his first speech took on that august and technically top-rank company of experts with a knowledgeable and valuable review of a century of British science, the notice was filled with sincere, if slightly apprehensive, respect.

The autumn of 1951 brought a testing job for the public partnership. Princess Elizabeth and Prince Philip were to sail in the *Empress of Britain* for a royal tour of Canada followed by a short visit to the United States. The original date of 25 September was postponed on account of the King's illness and operation. When the immediate post-operational danger was over and the new date had been fixed for 8 October, there was no time to go by ship, and Philip contrived to make it plain that if they could not fly the tour was off. Characteristically he seized the opportunity to break what seemed, in this age, the absurd embargo that his wife, as Heiress Presumptive, should not fly across the Atlantic. They went by BOAC Stratocruiser straight to Montreal, and have been flying around the world at intervals ever since.

The assignment was not an easy one. Originally it had been planned to be neither too long nor too arduous, but as usual the tour and the number of official stops had been expanded. Elizabeth was tired and tense after the strain of the previous weeks. As a daughter she was desperately anxious about a much-loved father, as Heiress Presumptive she had with her a sealed envelope containing the draft accession declaration, and a message to both Houses of Parliament, to be opened in the event of the King's death. It was not a happy situation, and added to her innate shyness it made Elizabeth appear withdrawn and unsure of herself. But Philip was there to help her along and add his own contribution of charm and laughter, to unbutton the protocol with his own brand of cheerful informality. Within days Elizabeth was relaxed and enjoying herself, and by the end of that ten-thousand-mile journey from east to west of the country, the pair of them had completely captured the affection of the Canadians.

It was the same when the tour was interrupted for a three-day visit to the United States. President Truman was so touched by Elizabeth's youth and sweetness as she made him a formal little speech on arrival, that he forgot protocol with a paternal, 'Thank you, my dear . . .' in reply.

The Americans liked this young, new-style royalty. They admired Elizabeth's 'quiet strength and serenity' and were appreciative of the 'intelligence and perception that lie beneath'. They enjoyed Philip's friendliness and easy informality, and sensing the tensions of constant publicity, forgave him when he used the rough edge of his tongue on a too-intrusive photographer.

In their turn Philip and Elizabeth liked America and the Americans. And if they found the scale of the security arrangements incomprehensible, Elizabeth did not seem to find the attentions of the American press quite as daunting as her daughter was to do eighteen years later. But then she had Philip to watch out for her, while Anne, except for her brother, who had Tricia Nixon as his vis à vis, was not provided with any male escort on her visit; and maybe Elizabeth, again unlike Anne, did not have two ladies of the press with notebooks at the ready, one at each elbow to interrupt impromptu remarks with, 'Would you just repeat that, honey? I didn't quite get it!'

When they arrived home again they found the King looking better, and delighted and proud with the triumph of an assignment that set the standard for all their overseas commitments of the future. He was to go in March with the Queen to recuperate in the warm sunshine of South Africa, after Philip and Elizabeth had set off again in the new year to represent him on a long tour taking in East Africa, Australia and New Zealand. In the meantime he was loving the companionship of his two small grandchildren and, at peace with the world, was looking forward to the years ahead when he could watch them growing up, and could coach Elizabeth even more minutely for the tasks of the future.

They were all at Sandringham for that Christmas, the King gay and carefree, confident of an eventual return to health, and utterly content as always when they were all together. He was so much better that there was a family theatre party at Drury Lane to see *South Pacific* at the end of January. The next day the King stood on the tarmac at London Airport, waving good-bye as Elizabeth and Philip flew off to Africa, and then returned to Sandringham to continue his holiday.

On 5 February the King was out shooting. It was a good day, a happy day, and he went to sleep tired and satisfied. In the early hours of 6 February King George vi died peacefully, without waking, at the home where he was happiest, secure in the love of his wife and family who were his life.

Coronation and public life

IN 1245 King Henry III ordered a great abbey church to be constructed at Westminster on the same site as another erected 150 years previously at the order of Edward the Confessor. In those days the public were admitted to the great churches only as pilgrims and on big occasions, but although the new edifice was primarily for the use of eighty monks, King Henry also designed his church as a fitting new shrine for the venerated bones of the saintly Edward, and as a suitable place for the crowning of his own successors. And with this end in view a deep space, called the Theatre, was left between the choir and steps leading up to the High Altar as an area to be used for coronations from that time onward.

Even before Westminster Abbey was built William the Conqueror, anxious to establish himself as Edward's legitimate successor, had begun the custom of English monarchs' being crowned on the same site. When Elizabeth II came to Westminster for her crowning it was the thirty-eighth coronation of a reigning sovereign, the twenty-eighth actually to have taken place in the Abbey.

Much had happened between the day in January 1952 when Princess Elizabeth and the Duke of Edinburgh left London Airport on the first leg of what was planned as a five-month tour of Kenya, Ceylon, Australia and New Zealand, and the solemn dedication of a Queen in Westminster Abbey little more than a year later.

They had flown on 31 January, a bleak grey day, leaving the King and Queen and Princess Margaret standing in a bitter wind to wave farewell, to touch down at Eastleigh Airport, Nairobi, less than twenty-four hours later, and step out into the brilliant African sunshine.

There was to be so little time before a sad message from England would change their world, that for Philip and Elizabeth those five days in Kenya must, in retrospect, appear as a kaleidoscope of quickly shifting scenes: huge crowds of ebullient Africans in robes of saffron, red, blue and green; Turkana warriors with ostrich-feather headdresses and capes of leopard skin; proud Masai, their headgear contrived from the manes of lions; twelve thousand children, Asian, African and British, all in their starched Sunday best assembled in the grounds of Government House to greet them; Indian girls from a local school, a colourful group beside the road, their saris shading from palest pink to grape purple. They remember the magnificent Askaris with their scarlet belts and tarbushes, who lined the route; the kilted band of the King's African Rifles beating the retreat after a garden party for more than two thousand people at Government House. There was the usual run of public duties and functions – visits to hospitals, a state dinner with the Governor, opening the Kenya Regiment's new headquarters, a service in the Cathedral of the Highlands, a civic reception at the City Hall.

There was an afternoon's safari in Nairobi National Park, with Elizabeth, who in those days did much of the photography, recording zebra, gazelle and wildebeest, giraffe, their improbable necks lovingly entwined, and a big-maned lion gorging himself on his kill. Then there was the peace and quiet of two days at Royal Lodge, the attractive single-storey house with its flower-filled garden, set in the foothills of Mount Kenya on the edge of the Nyeri Forest, which was Kenya's wedding present to them. There, both mornings not long after dawn they rode on a neighbouring farm, returning through a Kikuyu reserve, catching a glimpse of elephant crossing the track. Philip played polo at the Nyeri Polo Club, and in the evening they fished for trout in the Sagana River.

The next day they drove to Treetops, the original cabin, built high in a huge tree in the Abadare Forest game reserve.

On arrival there were the baboons to make Elizabeth laugh as they scrambled for the pea-nuts she threw down for them, but they were less intrusive than the baboon-ringleader Princess Anne encountered making for her bedroom when she visited the modern Treetops in 1970.

After dark when an artificial 'moon' highlighted the drinking pool and saltlick in the clearing down below their observation post, Philip and Elizabeth watched herds of elephant materialize silently out of the blackness of the forest, rhino lumber in to slake their thirst and two waterbuck that strove in and out of the shadows, their half-moon horns interlocked in battle. Several times during the few remaining hours of sleep the visitors, awakened by the snorts and grunts of new arrivals, crept out entranced to watch, but Philip can have had no inkling that the survival of animals like those riveting his attention on that night in 1952, would one day occupy much of his thoughts and energies as he endeavoured, with other people of vision, to conserve the world's wildlife.

Informal moments

At Badminton the Queen, watched by Edward and Andrew, takes photographs, while
Prince Philip and his eldest son carry on a conversation of their own

At a relative's
wedding, the Royal
Family for once betray
signs of impatience or
anxiety while waiting
for the bride (Princess
Alexandra) to arrive

The family all grouped together for the photographer
in the gardens at Windsor

First day for Prince Charles. His father shows him round
Gordonstoun, his old school

After the family race
down the course at
Ascot the Queen brings
carrots for her horse

After her family, the Queen's great love is for horses. Her
own race-horse Carrozza, ridden by Lester Piggott, wins
the Oaks at Epsom in 1957

The Queen out riding
with her sister,
Princess Anne and a
party of friends

Although on official
visits the Queen is
chauffeur-driven, she
prefers to drive her
own car round the
estates

Prince Philip flies his own helicopter which he lands in
Buckingham Palace grounds

It was a night of enchantment but one that in a few hours must have seemed like a dream, for in the early hours of the following day, all unknowingly Princess Elizabeth became Queen.

They left Treetops at 8.30 (it was three hours earlier in England) on the morning of 6 February and returned to Royal Lodge. The news of the King's death reached them after lunch and Philip was given the message by his equerry, his old friend Michael Parker. Philip told Elizabeth.

For many weeks Elizabeth and Philip, like all the royal family, had lived with the knowledge of the King's precarious hold on life, but however much thought is given to a contingency such as this, it makes no real impact on those concerned until it happens. This was the moment of truth for both of them. For Philip, a sudden facing of all the changes in their life that he had prayed would not come about for many a long day, and the bleak realization of what they could entail. But for Elizabeth it meant not only the abrupt assumption at a very early age of great responsibilities which were not hers by choice, but also the grief of losing a much-loved father. Only a very small part of Philip's grave concern would have been for himself.

Thunderstorms delayed the flight from Entebbe, but then very soon they were back at London Airport, where Mr Churchill and the leaders of the other two parties were waiting to greet their youthful, pathetically courageous Queen. There was the drive to Clarence House over which the royal standard was flying for the first time to bring home the reality, and almost immediately she was obliged to preside over a Privy Council, the first of the royal duties. For a girl may mourn her father but the Queen must be Queen. And if, as the King had felt, there was still so much he could have taught Elizabeth, given the time, he yet left her the fine legacy of her upbringing and his own example, and with them the courage and quiet, touching dignity that with Philip's loving support helped her face the first sad days.

On 8 February a fanfare of trumpets rendered by four state trumpeters called attention to Garter King of Arms, about to proclaim the new Queen from the balcony of St James's Palace. This statutory proclamation was read at three other points in London, at a number of towns and cities throughout Britain and the Dominions overseas, and aboard Her Majesty's ships 'wherever they might be'.

On 7 June another proclamation went out from St James's, Charing Cross, Chancery Lane and the Royal Exchange, 'Declaring Her Majesty's pleasure touching her Royal Coronation and the Solemnity thereof.' For this the arrangements were already in hand, under the auspices of the Coronation Commission with Prince Philip as chairman.

On 2 June 1953 at twenty-six minutes past ten o'clock, the Gold State Coach, weighing four tons, twenty-four feet long and 'the most superb and expensive of any built in this Kingdom', constructed for George III and decorated by the artist Cipriani, rumbled slowly out of the central gates of Buckingham Palace into a tumultuous greeting from hundreds of thousands of Her Majesty's subjects, wedged solidly along every inch of the processional route.

The coach was drawn, strictly at the walk, by eight Windsor greys caparisoned in state harness more than a century old, the four nearside animals controlled by bewigged postillions, aided if necessary by the fifteen footmen, similarly attired, attendant upon the entourage with some of the Yeomen of the Guard.

Before and behind rode or marched an impressive host – Admirals of the Fleet, Field Marshals, Marshals of the Royal Air Force; Sea Lords from the Board of Admiralty, Chiefs-of-Staff United Kingdom, escorts of officers from the colonial and Commonwealth contingents; those holders of resounding titles, Field Officers in Brigade Waiting, Gold-Stick-in-Waiting, Silver-Stick-in-Waiting, the Master of the Horse; personal and service aides-de-camp, equerries to the Queen, Yeomen of the Guard, the Queen's Bargemaster and Twelve Watermen; ten companies of Foot Guards, the Band and Corps of Drums of the Royal Horse Guards, and three Royal Grooms. This magnificent, glittering procession, to be augmented on its return journey with further detachments from the defence forces of the Commonwealth and Colonies and of the three services of the United Kingdom, wound its way down the Mall, past flags and decorative banners, beneath glistening arches (symbolic crowns suspended below, lion and unicorn rampant above), through Admiralty Arch, round Northumberland Avenue to the Victoria Embankment, and so across Parliament Square to Westminster Abbey. This was how the Queen, magnificently gowned and bejewelled, with Prince Philip beside her in the full-dress uniform of Admiral of the Fleet, came to her crowning sixteen months after acceding to the throne.

As coronation day drew nearer and for some while afterwards, a wave of emotionalism gripped the country. An unprecedented feeling of near-hysteria, quite different from the natural, warm enthusiasm and excitement to be expected, was centred on the Queen, born of the anti-climax of the post-war years superimposed on the long frightening period of hostilities.

No one could ignore such a flood of adulation, but few could have been better equipped to withstand being carried away by it, even to the smallest degree, than the central figure of the 'new Elizabethan era'.

The Queen is eminently practical. Everything she does and says demonstrates the honest, down-to-earth common sense of her nature, and there is, too, an odd aspect, a further shield against any fear of her 'having her head turned' at that, or any other time: she is totally without personal vanity, and while possessing a great sense of her position as Queen, she has little or none of herself as a person. Even now the Queen is still genuinely surprised by the size of the crowds she attracts, and remarks about people 'bothering' to come to see her.

Few sovereigns, least of all this true daughter of King George VI and his Queen, could come to their crowning without full consciousness and awe for its religious meaning and historical import, for all the weighty responsibilities involved and undertaken in the coming ceremony. The sense of dedication was strong as the Queen processed slowly up nave and choir to the Theatre, while the words of the anthem used since the coronation of Charles I, 'I was glad when they said unto me we will go into the house of the Lord ...' soared over the heads of the exalted company. Then in turn came the solemn rites of devotion and consecration, each with its own significance, scarcely changed in essence since 1689, beginning with the recognition and the ringing shout in answer: 'God Save Queen Elizabeth.' Then followed the anointing that is the spiritual climax, the giving of symbolic sword and ring, sceptre and rod, of the 'bracelets of sincerity and wisdom', a custom revived as emblems of the bond uniting the Queen and her peoples everywhere. And so to the investing, and at last the crowning with St Edward's crown, the great crown of England 'at sight whereof the people, with loud and repeated shouts, shall cry, God Save the Queen ... and the trumpets shall sound ... the great guns at the Tower be shot off'. And then towards the end came the homage, when Philip, first of the peers, ascended the steps of the throne to kneel, place his hands between the Queen's and declare: 'I, Philip, Duke of Edinburgh, do become your liege man of life and limb, and of earthly worship; and faith and truth I will bear unto you, to live and die, against all manner of folks. So help me God.' They were sincere words for all their ancient form, sincerely meant – and the same that their son, the little boy Charles brought for part of the service to sit with the Queen Mother and Princess Margaret, was to repeat to his mother sixteen years later when he was invested Prince of Wales.

ELIZABETH AND PHILIP

The triumphal progression back to the Palace, by a longer route which took in Whitehall and Pall Mall, Oxford Street and the Haymarket, was quite unmarred by the torrents of rain – through which Queen Salote of Tonga continued with her carriage open, sodden but unbowed, to the delight of everyone.

RAF Meteor jets screamed overhead in salute while the family watched from the balcony, and then repeated appearances to satisfy the clamouring crowds marked the end of the public side of coronation day. It was a day to remember in minutest detail, a devotional day for both of them, a day of promise and rejoicing, of dedication and elation – and a marathon of physical endurance.

The coronation confirmed the Queen in her life of service. It also set the seal on the third major phase in her life with Philip. First there had been the adjusting to each other's temperament common to all married couples, then the new parental role, and then with the accession the most difficult phase of all, when life with Philip as indisputable head of the family came not to an end but to a modification of its course.

When Philip married Elizabeth he had accepted that part of her life could never be his, and they had contended with this problem and started off their successful working partnership. But when Elizabeth became Queen so much earlier than anticipated, suddenly there were many others to take over where before there had been only Philip. Understandably some of those whose proud lifework is to help, advise and serve the throne, felt and showed little need for the aid of someone who is the Queen's husband but not the King, a consort in marriage and a prince by birth and right but, unlike Queen Victoria's Albert, not officially the Prince Consort.

It was not easy, but it was worked out together and in the meantime Philip, although he was certain of his ability to make more worthwhile contributions once an outlet had been found and anxious about Elizabeth's involvement, echoing Winston Churchill's words, 'I fear they may ask her to do too much,' restrained his natural impulsiveness, refrained from appearing too obviously the 'new broom', and slowly (for him) began fashioning his own position in the new regime.

All that is now a long time ago, and for many years the broom, no longer new, has been hard at work renovating this, dispensing with that, shaking up the other, stirring up controversies, all to his and Elizabeth's mutual satisfaction and enjoyment and, with only a few exceptions, to the common good.

CORONATION AND PUBLIC LIFE

Because all big issues are dealt with on the partnership basis and in close association with their advisers, it would be impossible to pin-point the exact originator of much that has been, and continues to be done to keep their way of life, as far as is desirable, in line with a changing world.

But Buckingham Palace is not the only place where some of the anachronisms have been weeded out without detracting from the overall picture. Heredity alone is no longer a passport to one of the four garden parties given annually at the Palace, functions that sprang, in the later stages of her reign, from Queen Victoria's natural desire to show off and present her big clan of children and grandchildren to society's upper crust. The world of the débutantes, which eventually became commercially debased and snob-ridden, is now mercifully erased. Nowadays the total of thirty thousand people a year who throng the Mall to gain entry, by invitation only, to the Palace and who have a much-valued chance to see some of the inside on their way to the gardens, dress in what they feel is appropriate to the occasion, and are there usually because they have been of some service to the community. In this manner the Queen and Prince Philip and usually other members of the family as well talk to as many people as possible – and that includes anyone from a town clerk or shop steward to an ex-prime minister, from a farmer or industrial chemist to students and servicemen from overseas.

The first of the informal luncheons was in 1956. The guests are chosen chiefly for their interest as people, and writers, teachers, explorers, artists, industrial barons and the like keep the Queen in touch with the many different aspects of modern life and enable her to meet more of the kind of people that Prince Philip knows from his enterprises. Much the same kind of cosmopolitan entertaining has gone into the cocktail parties and less formal dinner parties of recent years.

Between the accession and the end of 1971 the Queen and Prince Philip made twenty-one state visits and a great number of Commonwealth tours. It was the Australasian tour of 1970 that pioneered the new 'walkabout' idea which seemed to develop naturally out of the talks at different levels about the forthcoming programme in New Zealand. The Secretary of the New Zealand Internal Affairs Department and the Secretary to the Queen did the basic organization and set up the situations where a walkabout was possible. They did it so well, in fact, that the notion caught on and was welcomed as much by the Queen as by those who were able to speak to her.

It was not quite so welcome to the security organizations in Australia, where the thought of the Queen, walking down a main street packed with a hundred thousand people but without the usual weighty security arrangements, seemed more shocking than novel. Even after the proved success in New Zealand, the police of some of the Australian states had positively to be encouraged *not* to stand shoulder to shoulder, and to dispense with the troops normally called in to add their weight. Even then, the authorities in one city were so anxious about the experiment's taking place where they were responsible for the Queen's safety that although the Queen and Prince Philip and Princess Anne duly walked as planned, the old shoulder-to-shoulder formula was more than evident, and the Queen had to suggest they should find another place to try again the next day, but that there would really be little point in 'walking about' if the only people available for a friendly chat were uniformed police or soldiers!

At home it is now a matter of course that at some stage in each of the royal visits around the country the Queen and Prince Philip will be walking among the crowds quite informally; and this despite the bomb and assassination threats that have been stepped up in the last year or so.

There have always been a certain number of despicable threats of this nature, but the increase seems symptomatic of the age, and although the royal family take the only possible attitude – the threats have all proved to be hoaxes in the past so one works on the assumption this still applies – they realize that the police cannot afford to presume the same. The Queen and Prince Philip would never interfere with the degree of security or extent of precautions the police might think necessary, and would fall in with any steps taken for their safety that might be suggested, but their own immediate reaction is just to get on with the business in hand. Outwardly none of this appears to have any affect on them, but it must add something to the overall tension. If the crowds happen to know about it, it makes them that much more enthusiastic, that much more admiring in response, and unless the situation worsens there is no question of curtailing what is now one of the most popular of the 'public' innovations.

In their personal life the years have brought the Queen and Prince Philip the usual ups and downs and the increasing security and contentment shared by all those who are partners in a happy marriage. They have also brought, with the births of Andrew and Edward, the two younger boys, the completion of their family.

Family life

THE royal family are a very close-knit unit and really enjoy being together. They have the same 'goonish' sense of humour, and possibly
can relax completely on the same wavelength only in each other's
company, but the Queen's and Prince Philip's shared interests are
not all centred on their children. As a family they enjoy, and prefer,
the country existence possible at Windsor, Sandringham and Balmoral, but
the estates have to be administered in addition to being lived in, and Prince
Philip, who felt this was one load he could well carry for the Queen, took
over their supervision soon after the accession. Both of them get a great
deal of satisfaction and pleasure from all the rearrangements and reorganiza-
tion that have been going on ever since. They discuss the schemes for
turning Sandringham and the Home Farm at Windsor into economic
propositions – reclamation of land, new breeds of cattle and new crops
to try, enterprises like the bottling contract for fifty acres of blackcurrants,
the show successes with the Sandringham and Windsor herds making the
offspring that much more valuable in the market, as well as such ideas as the
redesigning of the garden at Windsor, completed some while ago, and the
forestry and general improvements that go on all the time in Scotland and
Norfolk.

Just occasionally the originator omits talking over a small plan with his
partner before putting it into operation. Then the Queen, riding in one of
the remoter corners of Sandringham or Balmoral, may come on some unexpected drainage or forestry operation and has sometimes to rely on one or
other of her younger sons, usually well versed in all that is going on, to
supply the required information so that she need not betray her ignorance!
If it comes to expostulating about the enclosure of good galloping ground
for cattle-grazing, the Queen can count on her daughter's support.

The role of a landowner means involvement with countryside pursuits
and with the lives and problems of all those who live on the estates. The
Queen and Prince Philip have a personal relationship with the tenants of
the numerous farms and cottages, and like to drop in for a friendly chat.

75

ELIZABETH AND PHILIP

This is the kind of life that appeals to them, and is one that provides contrast and relief from the formality of their public life.

Even during the Queen's official months in London the royal standard seldom flies over Buckingham Palace at weekends. Whenever possible Saturdays and Sundays, and most of the Easter holidays, are spent in the Castle at Windsor, built as a fortress by William the Conqueror and, like the Palace, state-owned.

When Windsor's towers and turrets are rose-tipped by the early morning sun and the massive walls below etherealized by lingering night mists, it has an enchantment too much like a fairy tale to seem real. But unlike many this castle has been lived in continuously since it was built, and although the beautiful state apartments and the treasures they contain are open to the public for most of the year, there is nothing of the soulless historic monument about Windsor. It is very much a lived-in home, and the Queen and her family love it.

Sheep and cows at the Home Farm, boats on the lake at Frogmore, the miniature cottage at Royal Lodge, polo at Smith's Lawn; occasional escapades, like Charles's and Anne's unpopular roof-top excursions to 'dong' the big bells on the tower clock; informal dances in St George's Hall, sessions of the 'Game' (a much-favoured if disconcerting version of charades); innumerable film shows, house-parties for Ascot, and the annual 'household' race on the course, inaugurated by the Queen as a girl and now dominated by Anne and her current escort; all these at times are part of the pattern of life at Windsor. And then, of course, once again there are the horses.

Except for the short interlude when Edward VIII replaced much of the actual horse-power with the mechanized variety, horses of many types have always been an essential part of Windsor. The big state-carriage animals, the Windsor greys, normally housed in the Royal Mews in London, derived their name from the four grey ponies that drew Queen Victoria's phaeton around the Windsor parks. Nowadays the numerous polo ponies (the majority belonging to the Household Cavalry), Anne's beloved Jinks and the riding and other horses in the Mews, combine the clatter of their hooves as they go to and fro, creating a characteristic background noise.

Another more intrusive sound is the roar and scream of the great jets coming in and out of Heathrow Airport, passing in succession in the skies above the Castle to bring conversation to a temporary halt. Although the wide reaches of the parks are criss-crossed with tracks sufficiently remote for riders to feel they are in the depths of the country, Windsor cannot provide the seclusion and privacy possible in Norfolk and Scotland, nor is it intended that it should. In this wonderful property, which belongs to the nation, the public have access to a large proportion of the beauties of Windsor, the Park and pictures, much of the interior of the Castle, and vistas like that of the grounds and building seen through the big gates leading to the Long Walk, which undulates dead-straight for a three-mile stretch used by royal vehicles only, leading to George III straddling the horizon on his copper horse. Because this public access is encouraged and welcomed, it seems all the more deplorable when, as has occasionally happened, a spying photographer with a telephoto lens manages to penetrate some of those areas which the royal family are entitled to enjoy in complete privacy – not that Windsor is the only field of operations for free-lance nuisances who make a living from 'candid' shots of royalty, and adds an indefensible strain to an already arduous life.

The gardens at Sandringham are open to the public for much of the year, and some of Prince Philip's more recent innovations have been to provide unobtrusive, grassy picnic-areas for the flocks of visitors who have permanent access to the woods and grounds outside the walls. But when the family move into the house for a few weeks after Christmas they have the grounds to themselves.

Sandringham, situated near the Wash, is, like Balmoral, the Queen's personal estate, and was bought in 1870 by Edward VII, then Prince of Wales. King George V loved it, and the Queen is reminded of her grandfather when she canters on the extra-wide verge he planned for exercising horses, between an avenue of trees and a three-mile stretch of road. King George VI was born in nearby York Cottage and ended his days as he would have wished, in the big house, the home where he always felt most happy and of which he wrote to Queen Mary: 'I want Lilibet and Philip to get to know it too...'

As he hoped, they and their children have always cared for this warm, cosy country-house, that seems made for dark evenings and big fires, games of hide-and-seek and the Christmas decorations that add to the family atmosphere. It is a real home where father and sons leave their outdoor shoes in the hall, and where Anne's bedroom is small and snug, full of cupboards and little different from the dressing-room it used to be. Until the house could no longer accommodate all the family and household who congregate at these times, Christmas was always spent at Sandringham, but now they stay at Windsor and go to Norfolk for a few weeks afterwards.

These are the times when the owners can do more than merely discuss the problems of the estate, and they enjoy plodding out in boots and mackintoshes to reconnoitre further improvements in person. The Queen likes to attend a meeting of the local Women's Institute, to watch her own labradors compete in gun-dog trials, and, unless frost forbids, to ride with Anne along the sheltered woodland tracks or out on the windswept fields. They meet country neighbours, and on most days the Queen joins her husband and elder son for a picnic lunch with the shooting party.

When he is at Sandringham Prince Philip may find the odd hour to paint an impression of the flat Norfolk countryside, to add to those watercolours of many parts of the world which he creates for his own pleasure and relaxation; but shooting is the main occupation at Sandringham. It was here that King George VI extended his future son-in-law's pleasure in the sport at which he himself excelled, and both Prince Philip and Prince Charles are first-class shots. In addition to the traditional Christmas holiday, father and son spend the occasional weekend at a farmhouse on the estate so that they can enjoy a Saturday shoot, and each year many thousands of wild pheasants are killed.

Like the cattle bred for the purpose and the surplus fruit, timber and any other marketable commodity, the birds, apart from a few brace, are sold to help defray the estate's running expenses. Amongst other very considerable items, these include the maintenance of over three hundred tenant properties, and the building and upkeep of a large number of pensioners' cottages. This is an aspect of the shooting to be considered by those who, with no real understanding of conservation, fail to reconcile Prince Philip's sport with his dedication to the properly controlled and knowledgeable preservation of wild animals. His critics might also find food for thought in comparing the accepted existence of a broiler chicken, and the life of a pheasant, allowed to mature in freedom and natural surroundings.

When she can the Queen also returns for a few additional days to Sandringham to see the new crop of foals. In her great-grandfather's time the adjoining stud was kept exclusively for breeding the royal thoroughbreds, and the huge, weatherbeaten statue of Persimmon, Edward VII's almost legendary racehorse, still dominates the paddocks and stabling. Nowadays the principal resident stallion is the well-known Ribero in which the Queen has a share, but except for a few royal thoroughbreds, the Duke's ex-polo ponies and one or two 'oddments' (perhaps animals related to one of the riding horses or bred as future carriage horses) most of the mares and foals belong to members of the public. So do most of those sent to the Queen's great horse, Auriole, which stands at the nearby Wolferton Stud, but sometimes one or two of the mares may also be the Queen's, along with their current foals by Auriole.

The Queen's well-known enjoyment of racing extends far beyond the normal thrills of the race-course. She does not bet, but is an owner and usually has about fourteen horses in training. The brood mares, foals and yearlings are divided between Hampton Court, headquarters of the royal thoroughbreds since Queen Victoria bred them there, and another nearby stud at Polhampton. Both studs are within easy reach of Windsor, and the Queen goes to see her horses when she can spare the time, showing an interest that is considerably more than academic. She has a wonderful 'eye for a horse' and a photographic memory – a foal seen at an early age will be recognized a year later with no trouble – and through the years she has studied the complicated subject of thoroughbred blood lines and breeding, until she is now one of the few acknowledged world experts.

When the Queen suggests to her racing manager that one of her mares should go to some particular stallion he accepts the proposal without question – not because she is the Queen, but because he knows she really understands her subject. In fact, the Queen works out all the mating programmes for her brood mares, and in subsequent years has the fun and excitement of following the careers of animals resulting from her decisions. During the flat-racing season she is in constant direct communication about her horses, telephoning her trainers to discuss progress, training and racing schedules, and results.

This hobby is one that the Queen does not share with husband or family. Prince Philip, like his daughter, much prefers taking part in a sport to being a spectator. His enthusiasm for racing is limited – appearances with the Queen at the big occasions of the racing calendar have often been curtailed so that he could fit in a game of polo – and he is happy to leave the intricacies of thoroughbred horse-breeding to his wife.

The Duke has his own particular interests, most of them now so interwoven with some facet of his job that they are no longer strictly in the category of hobbies. The painting remains one of them, but nature photography, which grew from the purchase of an expensive camera and a casual try-out with sea-birds in 1956, is now bound up, to some extent, with his involvement in the World Wildlife Fund, of which he is an international trustee. His love of sailing and racing small boats, instilled when at school at Gordonstoun, had a high priority for many years. It was easy enough when he was in the Navy, and for the short while when he and, at intervals, Elizabeth were based on Malta soon after their marriage. Later there were wonderful seasons of racing regularly at Cowes with his friend Uffa Fox, but in 1971 when the Duke and Charles and Anne were at Cowes together, although Prince Philip put up an excellent performance in an unfamiliar 'Daring' class yacht to come third in one of the Royal Yacht Squadron regatta events, most of the racing was undertaken, with some success, by the Prince of Wales. Prince Philip used to take his elder children sailing on the Scottish lochs when they were quite young, and these trips were extended when they took the yawl *Bloodhound* (since sold) on happy excursions exploring the west coast of Scotland, hooking up anywhere they happened to be for the night, and setting off again to cruise from A to B the next day if they felt like it.

They take to the sea as a family, if, as often happens, the holiday starts off with a cruise in the royal yacht *Britannia,* that lands them eventually in Scotland. Life on board means real freedom to relax, to dress as they please, to indulge in the hearty type of deck-game that is a family pastime. There is no publicity, no 'best behaviour', no formality, no work – except for the Queen, when the frequent helicopter brings in the state papers – and they can enjoy the much appreciated, traditional hospitality of the Royal Navy.

In Scotland the Queen still has affairs of state to attend to, daily sessions with the Private Secretaries, and at intervals important government and other guests to entertain, but otherwise the life at Balmoral is equally carefree. This is the chief reason why this small Scottish castle, which was built and much loved by Queen Victoria and the Prince Consort, remains the favourite home.

Some of the pattern of the days is familiar. There are horses and ponies to ride, grouse to shoot instead of pheasants, gun-dogs to work, picnic lunches with the guns to enjoy, and always life in the open air, for all of them, regardless of weather. For those who like it, there is also the physically arduous, skilled art of stalking, and the knowledge of the ways of the red deer that goes with it.

FAMILY LIFE

Each morning and evening Anne, no fonder of walking than her father, shoots off on a bicycle carrying headcollars to bring in or take out the horses, then to ride to or from the paddock bareback on High Jinks, her original pony who is now practically a member of the family, with three or four others led at either hand. Sometimes after tea Edward will come dashing out of the side-door on his bicycle, to join Andrew and race their Snowdon cousins in the go-karts, the phut-phutting of the engines shattering an atmosphere more tuned to the skirl of the pipes. They bank perilously round the lawns, their heads protected by very necessary crash-helmets, and miss each other by seconds on the narrow paths that criss-cross between the Castle and the stable yard. Anne may come to demonstrate her speciality, skid-turns in a cloud of dust on the gravelly drive, or to challenge Charles to a race. Young cousin David, missing the cornice of a stone balustrade by an inch, is showing the same penchant for speed that worries the groom-in-charge when the children go out riding. There is a change to bicycles, and the clatter of a crash round one of the corners brings an equerry on the run from the room where he works, just inside the door. But satisfied there is more noise than damage, he quickly retreats inside once more.

Some evenings everyone musters to build a giant bonfire and join in a sing-song with perhaps a few fireworks in the dusk, but whatever the diversion, it is nearly always enjoyed by children and grown-ups together.

Frequently about midday, two big Land Rovers, or a kind of bus if the houseparty is a large one, are parked outside the main door. Family and guests appear, children, dogs and hampers are piled in, the Queen may climb into one driving seat, Charles take the other and they are off. The cars swoop down the valley, pause for a call to the horses grazing in the paddock, then roar out of the grounds and up on to the hill.

Queen Victoria used to drive along this route, the carriage bumping along the tracks, then rough and unmetalled, that snake between lichen-covered boulders and peaty hags, mounds of purple heather and drifts of white-tufted cotton-grass, all chequered by cloud shadows chasing across the moors. When her carriage overturned that intrepid lady noted in her diary: 'We had only a little claret with which to mop up the blood.' This laconic attitude appeals to the Queen, who has much affection for that great-great-grandmother whose personality is still so evident at Balmoral.

If the picnic-party end up at Loch Muick, one of their favourite haunts, they come to that solitary little house that Queen Victoria had built beside the water, on a spit of land she never paid for, so that King George VI had eventually to find the money.

There is a strip of grass between the house and the loch edge, and on it through the years a battalion of scotch firs have grown up and marched almost to one wall so that the small rooms are dim and rather eerie. The Queen keeps the interior exactly as it was the last time her great-great-grandmother closed the door to leave, and renews the same wall-paper, the same patterned curtains and bed-flounces. Even the musical box has been mended to tinkle out the same little tunes that entranced that other Queen so long ago.

Outside, where one minute the sun turns the loch face to crystal, and the next looming clouds match water to the dark mountain plunging straight down on the opposite shore, there is a hustle of activity. The iron barbecue is fetched from the house, charcoal kindled and coaxed to a glow, the cars are unpacked and the raw materials brought over for one of Prince Philip's culinary specialities. Then, while he gets busy with the cooking that is his hobby and Anne acts as assistant chef, the Queen makes a salad, Charles concocts the dressing, others deal with the rest of the meal, the dogs chase rabbits, and the children chase the dogs or squabble happily amongst themselves.

It is all very gay and simple and the main rites scarcely change with the years. Occasionally the children want to bring a boat for rowing on the loch, and then a trailer is hitched behind one of the cars to transport a light, aluminium craft belonging to Andrew. Sometimes they drive home soon after eating, sometimes spend hours in this lovely spot, or at one of the others dotted about the estate that are also popular places for picnicking.

At some time after arriving back at Balmoral the Queen will call the dogs and tramp off by herself around the grounds for one of the walks she takes daily whenever possible, alone except for her corgis. The ritual is easy enough at Balmoral and Sandringham, but the solitude is not quite so assured in London now. The Palace gardens are large enough to accommodate in comfort the eight or nine thousand guests attending a royal garden party, but there are few corners that are not now overlooked by the windows of skyscraper buildings. At Windsor the Queen sometimes slips across the lawn and goes through the high archway into the Middle Court of the Mews where her horses are housed. She chooses a time when there is no one else around but the friendly creatures she has come to see, and in their undemanding company feels the same re-charging of the batteries of the mind she obtains from her solitary walks.

To be alone at intervals is very important to the Queen, as essential to her nature as to live mostly at full stretch is to Prince Philip's. As always, these and all the other facets of their personalities owe something to the Queen's and Prince Philip's ancestry, to their youth and upbringing, and to all the pleasures and pressures of their days.

Private pursuits and interests

Most of Prince Philip's and Charles's riding activities are to do with Polo. *Above*, they are playing at Smith's Lawn, where Prince Philip captained the Windsor side

Left Prince Philip receiving the gold cup and a smile from his wife

Family chat and jokes after a strenuous game

Her father didn't believe she could do it but Princess Anne did ride for Britain in the European Event championships

Princess Anne and Prince Andrew with their father at the Badminton horse trials

Right The Queen and Prince Philip at the royal farm and with their farm manager

Far right Prince Philip driving his family back from a visit to the Scilly Isles

Like father, like son

People normally think of Prince Philip as an outdoor person, but he is also interested in photography and finds relaxation in painting

Prince Philip and Princess Anne share a love of cookery

Family lunch at Windsor Castle. Prince Charles and his father with their hands folded and their heads tilted to one side, in exactly the same way. *Opposite top* The younger children are always up to something. The Queen and Prince look anxious as they wonder whether the boys will make it up the side of the bridge, but their father has no such qualms

Right Two charming portraits of
the Queen with her youngest son,
Prince Edward, as a baby and Prince
Andrew

Family interests

THE Queen does not consider herself 'horsey', she just loves horses. This is an accurate assessment, and the distinction is bigger and less subtle than some might imagine. Nor has her interest anything to do with 'snob' value. Her famous ex-racehorse Auriole is a priceless thoroughbred and sire of worldwide repute and the Queen is rightly very proud of him, but for years the top favourite amongst her riding horses was Betsy, a mare with considerably more personality than blue blood. Horses of many different shapes, sizes and types are an intrinsic part of royal life, and provide much of the essential relaxation and escape.

When Charles and Anne were still quite young and their father's leisure-time more extensive, parents and children sometimes rode out as a foursome, and Prince Philip still occasionally joins some of his family out riding. But soon polo, practice and actual games, began to occupy any time the Duke might have to spare for hacking, and Charles found new interests at school, his riding possibly discouraged for a time by the extra keenness and talent shown by a sister younger than himself and prone to offering unsolicited advice. (Use your *legs*, Charles!)

Although the Queen says she leaves the finer arts of equitation to her daughter, she has the instinctive rapport with horses that is the mark of the true horseman. She loves to ride and does so whenever she can. But for several years, apart from her own riding and the polo interest shared with her husband, the Queen's extraneous horse activities at Windsor were mostly centred on Anne. Then, when he was about fifteen, Charles suddenly became polo-conscious too, and before long the Queen found herself with both husband and son equally enthusiastic, if then at very different levels, over the rough, thrilling game she wishes she could play herself.

With two members of one family participating regularly in what is ad-mittedly a dangerous sport there are bound to be occasional crashes and injuries, but the Queen and her family are philosophical about these things, and accept that the element of risk attached to most strenuous activities adds to the excitement.

G

ELIZABETH AND PHILIP

When someone suggested it was madness to have allowed Prince Charles to play polo on the Sunday before his investiture as Prince of Wales, the Queen was genuinely amazed because she had never given it a thought. Obviously she believes that reasonable precautions should be taken over her family's more hazardous amusements, and the calm capability of Princess Anne's trainer, Mrs Oliver, and a horse that can really jump, have done much to allay natural parental anxieties about Anne's Eventing. As a family they do not 'fuss', and the Queen takes the rational outlook shared by them all, that it is just as possible to fall out of bed and suffer injury that way!

Her family seem to take it for granted that the Queen should contribute to their polo-playing by being chief 'stomper-in' of the divots that fly from the hooves of galloping ponies. This duty does not just entail getting to work between chukkas during a match on Smith's Lawn, where younger children are usually available to help, but has always included the urgent repairs necessary after husband or son have had one of their frequent practice sessions on the lawn at Windsor.

Most of the facilities for the various outdoor diversions at Windsor seem to be at close quarters. The Queen has had some anxious moments riding in the Home Park when Prince Philip has decided to bring down a noisy helicopter on to the landing pad just behind where Anne used to have her practice show-jumps. The Duke could sometimes be seen, and heard, emerging with a polo pony from the depths of one of the bunkers belonging to the adjacent nine-hole golf course – the scene of an incident some years ago when the Queen *did* delegate turf repairs to her daughter. That was the day when Anne hoisted the new nursery-maid on to the back of an Arabian horse, presented to the Queen by King Hussein, and Pride carted his unwilling rider in a bee-line for stable and lunch, straight across one of the golfing greens. It was an unpopular moment, but despite the Queen's comments, which brooked no argument as to *who* was going to make good *that* damage, there are still frequent occasions when Anne has to be implored to remove some horse or other off the lawn.

Polo, which until he gave it up at the end of the 1971 season, Prince Philip played whenever he got the chance, is admirably suited to his temperament. The speed and toughness of the game provided opportunities to work off tensions and superfluous energies, the violent exercise helped keep him physically fit, and the single-minded determination to go in and win (a competitive quality his daughter shares) allied to a natural 'eye for the ball', helped make him one of the top-ranking players in the world. It must have been a wrench to give polo up, but the Duke had said for some time that he might when he reached his fiftieth birthday and recurring trouble with a damaged wrist confirmed his decision. Nowadays he keeps a connection with polo by occasionally umpiring a game. It is possible that he will begin to devote more time to leisure riding again to make up for the exercise he must miss.

The Duke always took an interest in his ponies apart from the game, but lacked quite the same relationship with them that the Queen, Charles and Anne have with their horses. He used to call in at Prince Philip's Yard, part of the Windsor Mews where the ponies are kept, to discuss them and their welfare, but in play, intense keenness and an innate impatience made it difficult for him to give due allowance to young or inexperienced animals. He liked them instantly responsive to his own riding methods, and as near possible to the standard set by Betaway, that thoroughbred pony, retired to stud at Sandringham, who was so handy and fast she became a by-word. When Prince Philip opened the throttle and let Betaway go even top-notch players gave up trying to catch them.

Betaway is not the only polo-pony to become a brood mare at Sandringham, and the Queen has always been hopeful that some of the resultant offspring might be suitable for some of the family players. Unfortunately this is one side of her horse-breeding with which the Queen has little luck. Prince Philip seldom, if ever, seemed to get on terms with the home-bred ponies, Prince Charles's string is usually conspicuous by their absence, and a number grow too big for the game anyway. The Queen has found one or two of the rejects admirable for pleasure-riding, and although Prince Philip teases her about the 'outsizes', suggesting their growth is due to being too well fed, one called Doublet hit the headlines in 1971, when Princess Anne rode him to trounce the top riders from nine countries and become the Individual Three-Day Event champion of Europe.

This story has its roots in those days when the Queen used to enjoy driving her car in pursuit of Anne and a crowd of other children and ponies, scampering around the parks at Windsor on a mounted paper chase, or negotiating miniature horse-trial fences. Those were the same inviting little jumps, set around the perimeter of the golf course, over which the Queen once led a posse of unsuspecting guests, riding the royal horses and in honour bound to follow, whatever their standard of horsemanship!

ELIZABETH AND PHILIP

As time went by, with the co-operation of her pony High Jinks and the good instruction they both received during school years, Anne's enthusiasm and aptitude for jumping and cross-country riding increased, and her successes, at Pony Club level, began to multiply. When she left school the Princess was determined to see if she could make her mark in the very different world of adult competition.

She could have gone to some famous equestrian school to learn the art of Eventing as painlessly as possible; she could have bought some famous, winning Event horse to 'schoolmaster' her first efforts, but Anne is never one to take the easy way out and has an inherited like of doing things for herself. So Alison Oliver, wife of the well-known show jumper, agreed to help, and the Queen loaned her daughter a young, inexperienced horse, home bred from one of Prince Philip's ex-polo ponies and by a stallion that came from the Argentine to race in this country.

Mrs Oliver has a rare skill for training rider and horse as a unit, but in this case she is the first to say she was very lucky with her pupil, and right from the start it was a combined effort. There was never a hint of a rich young girl arriving with all the required equipment, and expecting to have her horse trained for her so that all she had to do was to climb on top and press the correct buttons at the right moment.

Riding and achievement in this particular branch of the sport are of real importance to the Queen's daughter, and not only for the enjoyment she gets out of it. This is one way she can prove to herself, as well as to other people, that her position in life is unrelated to any success she may attain. If she is good at riding, she is good at it, and it has nothing to do with the fact that she happens to be Princess Anne.

This is much the same outlook that motivates many of Prince Charles's activities, that urges him to take on the extras such as making a parachute drop that was not strictly officially necessary. It is the same emphasis on the man, not the prince, that has been Prince Philip's incentive all his life.

When it comes to riding Anne has a big asset in that, like the Queen, she is very quick to understand and apply what is required of her, but both she and Doublet had a great deal to learn. As a Princess she had not only to achieve the high standard of horsemanship, and the necessary philosophical approach of accepting that a horse will win one day and fail the next, but also to deal with the extra difficulties allied to her position. Because of her commitments she always has much less time for training than is the case with

88

the majority; she has had to withstand the exceptional and increasing pressures and tensions of publicity, photographers, and over-enthusiastic spectators; and at first there was the need to persuade the members of the Eventing world to accept her as one of themselves, on merit alone. She succeeded and continues to do so because she is not afraid of concentrated hard work and has the determination, the right competitive spirit, and the 'guts', that are some of the essential qualities.

By the time she was nineteen and already well and successfully embarked on her public life, Anne was even more keen and ambitious about Eventing, and Alison Oliver was secretly convinced of both the rider's and the horse's potential. The Queen, more than interested in both Anne and Doublet, could not fail to understand her daughter's dedication, and their common love of horses has always been a great bond between them; but she is not the first mother to have felt it might be a good thing if other diversions could be developed as well. This was a hope that Prince Philip was bound to share. He feels very strongly that young people should write themselves some sort of worthwhile record in life to look back on, and could not then visualize riding as quite fitting the bill – especially as even the thought of competing at international level, seemed to him at the time to be aiming a bit high! To everyone, with the possible exception of Princess Anne and her trainer, that day less than two years ahead when she and Doublet would come fifth overall at the Badminton Horse Trials, one of the toughest competitions in a tough sport, a first attempt at a Three-Day Event, must have seemed a remote chance. Their victory, in the European Championships at Burghley in the same year, and as it happened only a couple of months after the Princess had had a serious operation, would have appeared real 'pie in the sky'.

But there was nothing unreal about that sunny day early in September 1971 when Prince Philip stood waiting with his daughter, at the start of the Cross-Country phase of a Three-Day Event that is not far below Olympic standard. Anne, already well in the lead after a first-class Dressage Test, had just put eleven miles of roads and tracks and a two-mile steeplechase safely behind her. Then she was away, and there was the Queen jumping out of an estate car at various points on the four-and-three-quarter-mile course, just in time to see her daughter and horse negotiate yet another of the thirty-three formidable obstacles, some of Olympic dimensions. And at the end the Queen and Prince Philip were to learn Anne had come in clear, at a speed that made it the second fastest time of the competition.

It only needed the clear round over the show jumps on the final day to clinch the victory, and fill the cup of parental delight and pride to overflowing. Their sentiments were shared by the sporting and non-sporting world alike, and they were expressed by the Queen and Prince Philip in their unmistakable excitement and the big kiss they both gave their daughter after she received her trophy.

And what a triumph it was, to finish thirty-eight points ahead of the runner-up, beating the best of the riders in Europe when one is only twenty-one, relatively inexperienced in the sport concerned, and out to prove oneself in one's own eyes and to the world at large.

To ride for Great Britain in the 1972 Olympics was the Princess's next obvious and admitted ambition, one in which the Queen and Prince Philip wholeheartedly concurred, but even if Anne had been selected for inclusion in Britain's Eventing Team at Badminton in 1972, as she well knew there was still a long way to go before Munich. And as it happened her luck was out and Doublet went lame.

Whatever happens in the future, his daughter's accomplishments to date must surely qualify for what Prince Philip considers a demonstrable achievement. No doubt Anne will continue Eventing at various levels with various horses as her sport – and she has already included two young novice home-bred horses in her string – but there is only the one step higher, the Olympics, left in this particular sphere, and she does not appear likely to rest on her laurels. Before long the Queen and Prince Philip may be encouraging their daughter in whatever fresh fields she sets out to conquer, whether in her public life, her personal ambitions, or both.

Educating the royal children

THE idea that the royal family should, as a family, strengthen the throne and set an example by the character and behaviour of its various members, started to emerge only during the Victorian era. Before then many of the royal ménages were distinctly irregular, to put it mildly, and of those few people outside the court circle who would actually have known anything of the private life of the monarch and his family, fewer still would have noted or cared what course it took.

Today, as Prince Philip says, one of the assets of the monarchy is that it does involve a whole family, so that different age groups are part of it, and some people can look to the Queen Mother and identify themselves with her generation, others with the Queen and himself, and others with their children.

Although in this last case many of the young of today would never confess to 'looking up' to anyone, and certainly Princess Anne used to appear aghast at the thought of being cited as an example, she and Prince Charles, and their younger brothers in turn, consciously or unconsciously have an effect on a proportion of their own generation, simply by being the people they are and by doing the things they do; and what they are and what they do have roots in their upbringing and in the pattern of life set them by their parents.

Most parents grow more relaxed in their attitude to succeeding children, particularly at the nursery age, and possibly Andrew and Edward have profited by this tendency. There are eighteen months between Charles and Anne, then a ten-year age gap between Anne and Andrew, with Edward four years younger still, so that the children have been brought up in two distinct groups.

The elder two had a typically conventional nursery regime for the first few years. The emphasis on being 'good', clean and tidy was so obviously inherent in their then nanny's outlook that Anne, anyway, attached no special significance to it all, since it was 'just life'. Under Mabel Anderson's rule the basic routine was unchanged but otherwise there was increasing freedom, and it was symptomatic that jeans and jerseys became standard everyday wear. There has never been any spoiling; good manners, thought for others and obedience have always been instilled, and an occasional spanking or other suitable punishment meted out when necessary, but the nursery has engendered the same easy, happy atmosphere that the children have always enjoyed with their parents.

Charles was an amenable, sensitive little boy, shy but with an apparently built-in awareness of what was required of him, and from the earliest age a far more 'certain starter' in public than his less predictable sister. Anne was a lovable, affectionate child too, but a born ringleader, inclined to boss, with an adventurous 'try-anything-once' attitude and the capacity to throw tempestuous if short-lived scenes when thwarted. Those tantrums were reserved for the nursery, and are recalled today when Edward, of somewhat similar temperament, occasionally sticks his toes in.

The Queen and Prince Philip appear to have the enviable ability to quell their children when young with little more than a word or look. The Queen is adept in such matters as steering a laggard small boy, bent on skilful delaying tactics, firmly but tactfully towards bed, and she remembers Anne as an ordinarily easy little girl, if perhaps more moody than the boys. But, looking back, Prince Philip thinks that as quite a small child his daughter did resent being a girl, and being second in the family, with an elder brother who was, in their nanny's eyes, of more importance, and that even when she was not old enough to register her emotions, she felt herself in some way neglected. Their parents made no material difference between the two children, but Anne can still recall her sense of outrage when Charles was taken to Westminster Abbey to see a small part of their mother's crowning, and as only a three-year-old she was left behind to watch the procession from the Palace balcony with some other little girls, the type of company for which she had no use anyway!

Then Charles went to school, first daily to the same brand of pre-prep-school that Edward started at in the autumn of 1971, then to Cheam, his father's old prep-school. Anne stayed at home to continue lessons with Charles's governess.

Now that brother and sister are grown up the difference in their characters is even more apparent. But though they still argue about most things and go their separate ways, they much enjoy each other's company when they are together, and share a similar sense of humour that can be near-fatal should they catch each other's eye at a public function. Sailing, driving fast cars, life in the open air are mutual pleasures, but although Charles is as much in his element flying as his father, Anne's ears refuse to attune to this type of travel and she considers a horse the only kind of transport guaranteed not to make her feel sick! Charles loves music, concerts and operas, the theatre, and looking at pictures, none of which have much appeal for Anne. Like many brothers and sisters they have a totally dissimilar set of friends.

In those years long ago when Charles as a young boy had seemed so unsure of himself, so dependent on people and companionship, Anne in her determination to keep up with an elder brother always appeared much tougher and completely self-confident. Then, if someone had shown Charles how to do something, he would probably have said: 'Yes, I see now, thank you so much for showing me ...' Anne would have been more likely to remark, 'Thank you – but I know ... !'

In general she was on good terms with her governess and it is only in retrospect, having known something of freedom since, that Anne realizes how comparatively restricted life was in those early years. But even so, it began to irk increasingly that there was no escaping someone whose duty it was always to know where she was and what she was doing. There were daydreams of living in another age, always as a country girl of no account, with a 'let-be' existence, free as air. By the time she was twelve she was already sick of home lessons, wanting to stretch her wings in the company of different people, in a different environment, and ready to jump at her parents' suggestion that she should go to boarding school in the autumn of 1963.

This was a totally new departure for a British princess, but the Queen and Prince Philip realized that further home education would be poor preparation for life in a modern world. Yet although Anne thoroughly enjoyed her years at school, after the first shock of community life and ceaseless noise had worn off, and seized on the opportunity to become just one of the crowd, the Queen is not certain that boarding school provided all the answers. Certainly when Anne first left school, and before she began her public life and had found her feet as an adult, it was not easy to return to the royal restrictions – especially at a moment when her friends and contemporaries were striking out with their own flats and jobs and independent existences.

Fortunately their daughter has inherited the Queen's and Prince Philip's philosophical ability to accept life as it is, and she set out to discover just how much could be done within the limits rather than wasting time and energies envying the unattainable. Her objective appears, in many ways, to have been successfully achieved.

At different stages of their children's upbringing the Queen and Prince Philip have received a great deal of gratuitous public advice. There were articles in the press and magazines to tell them how right, or how wrong, they were to send their eldest son to Prince Philip's old school Gordonstoun. At one time the Queen was being begged to allow her daughter to dress like others of her age group, and was implored almost in the same breath to stop Princess Anne from appearing in such dreadful 'way-out' clothes. Even today there are entreaties to a nebulous 'they' to release Anne from all public duties so that she need do nothing but ride horses. But the pundits tend to miss the point.

The Queen and Prince Philip think that one of the many things parents should not do is to try to mould their children into becoming people different from what, intrinsically, they are, and that they can be encouraged, but not coerced, to do the kind of things that may stand them in good stead in the future. They themselves follow the commendable practice of putting the pros and cons of matters concerning their older children to them, and then leaving them to make up their own minds. The policy is no doubt beginning to operate with Andrew, and will be employed in due course with Edward.

The Queen and Prince Philip seldom give a categorical 'yes' or 'no' once the children are old enough to make sensible decisions, a course of action that Anne found 'very valuable' as a teenager. Apart from other considerations it put a break on 'making a fool of oneself', because there would be no one else to blame!

Charles was not *sent* to Gordonstoun, he was given the alternatives and asked if he would like to go. As Heir Apparent he had borne the full brunt of press and public over-attention during the first weeks at Cheam, and possibly the remoteness and inaccessibility of Gordonstoun influenced his decision to a degree. Possibly as one of his father's chief admirers, if in character more like his mother and grandmother, Charles typically accepted the challenge of following in his ebullient father's footsteps, because he realized the going would be rough – the old necessity to prove oneself to oneself. It was a tough but in the main a successful choice and, like his father, Charles became Guardian of the school, strictly on merit. But the most weighty factor would have been the one that is the guiding principle in this young man's life. He subscribes fully to Prince Philip's idea that the royal family should count, in

EDUCATING THE ROYAL CHILDREN

National Insurance parlance, as self-employed, with the necessity for working to justify their keep. With a sensitive, deep awareness of the responsibilities that may one day be his, Charles will do and take on those things he considers most likely to make him competent to deal with his mission in life.

In the years since leaving school no doubt the path he has followed – Cambridge; the Australian interlude (those two terms at Timbertops remain among the highlights); the brief stay at University College, Aberystwyth; the short term of service in the Air Force – was suggested and discussed at length, but in each case his would have been the final decision, just as it would have been Charles himself who opted for a naval career, despite his aptitude for flying and the previous experience that helped him complete, in five months, the standard twelve-month course for entry into the RAF through Cranwell, and despite the citation, 'above the average', that went with his Wings.

Probably family custom played a part here. For although George VI was the first English king to hold a pilot's licence and wear an airman's badge, and in spite of the example of a father who is considerably happier flying a helicopter, or one of the forty-seven other types of aircraft within his range, than tramping anywhere on his two feet, the naval tradition is stronger yet. His father, his grandfather and uncles on the paternal side, and both George V and George VI on the Queen's, were at one time and another all serving naval officers. But once again the most important element would be that history has proved naval training a good aid to becoming a worthwhile king, and Charles would welcome the discipline that enlarges the self-control both he and Anne consider essential to an ordered existence.

When her daughter was young the Queen chose her clothes from the pretty but not over-exciting selection then in vogue for small children. When Anne was about fourteen she and Mabel began going out to the shops to bring back ready-made clothes on approval, and the Queen never vetoed anything that was particularly liked. Even when Anne suddenly became conscious of clothes and her own appearance, shed unbecoming plumpness by eating less and riding horses further and harder in the course of her hobby, and then started to experiment with the trendy gear of the age, apart from the occasional plea, her mother never attempted to exert any influence. At the very beginning, before Anne fully developed her distinct flair for clothes that are both attractive and 'with it', it must occasionally have called for some restraint on the Queen's part. For after all, even if 'oxford bags', and the flappers' daringly short skirts that went with their non-existent waists and Eton-cropped heads were the 'in' thing when the Queen was born, by the time she was Anne's age tweedy coats and calf-length skirts with sensible brogues were recognized country wear, and the then fashions in town would scarcely be described nowadays as daring, or any preparation for some of the modern trends.

The 'advisers' most off the beam are those who reckon that Princess Anne should be 'let off' her public duties. The Queen and Prince Philip have their working partnership, and George VI's saying: 'We're not a family; we're a firm,' is as true of this generation as it was of his. This is something of which Anne is very conscious. She may sometimes kick a little against the limitations and she is determined on finding time to take her Eventing seriously, but it is just not part of her nature even to contemplate opting out of her share in the obligations. Like her father she does not consider that the ability to do public duties well rates as a gainful achievement, and is building her interest and efficiency around the Save the Children Fund as one very worthwhile project. But public commitments are one of the duties required of royalty, and by playing her part in this side of royal life Anne is also helping out her mother, for whom she has the deepest love and admiration.

When she first began her public life the Princess shared one of the Queen's ladies-in-waiting, and consulted her mother about any commitments she felt she might undertake. Now, like Charles, she has her own office and staff in the Palace, and enjoys the same almost curiously independent working life. As a family they always thoroughly enjoy the engagements and visits abroad together, and family matters are always discussed fully as a family, but when it comes to public functions performed separately which it would seem could hardly fail to be mentioned, quite often these get left out of the conversation, and then it suddenly transpires in their various offices that the family are totally unaware of one another's assignments!

During 1969 the Queen and Prince Philip watched with some natural pride and their usual down-to-earth attitude the headlined enthusiasm with which press and public greeted Charles on his emergence into the public eye, and Anne, when she embarked on her 'first time round'. The Queen was happy that their first year should go so well. The Duke, tongue in cheek, felt that his children's news-value was due partly to the public's discovery that these two young people were both attractive and normally intelligent! Anne, feet as usual well on the ground, assessed the excitement principally as novelty-rating, but she was genuinely moved by the warmth of the reception she got in places such as Newcastle, and expressed surprise that the interest seemed to be continuing.

Since then Charles has developed his early promise of becoming a witty and exceptional speaker, and if a small proportion of his generation choose to appraise him as 'square', the majority of people of all ages and both sexes respect his sincere and engaging concern for the other man's point of view and way of life.

The second time round Anne ran into a little rough weather, some in Australia, more in America. As with her father, protocol is not one of her favourite words, and added to a strong preference for participation rather than the static role of onlooker is the inability of a very honest personality to make much success of dissembling. No doubt at times Anne was bored and tired, but she also shares the family features that, in repose, can make the Queen look unduly solemn when she is in fact merely intent.

With experience Anne is becoming more aware of the royal necessity for treading warily, but combines it with her father's aptitude for speaking his mind at intervals, and has a quick response for anyone who makes her laugh. She cannot as yet shrug off with quite the same equanimity as her parents the occasional press report that is not only untrue but hurtful, but that comes with the years. She is learning to deal with the strange, sudden embarrassment in the presence of royalty, that can descend on people at the most unlikely moments. This is something to which the Queen is now inured, even though, sadly, it can inhibit her from pleasures like going to visit Andrew at school as often as she would like because people at once become 'different', and that would be unfair to such an extrovert character as her second son.

Like most young people Anne tends to take a back seat when with members of her family on public engagements, but rises to the occasion when out on her own. The film of her visit as president of the Save the Children Fund to Kenya in 1970, made by the BBC for their programme 'Blue Peter', illustrates this point, and gives a very true picture of the Princess's unaffected, intelligent approach. That film also demonstrated Anne's rapport with children, a fact that never ceases to surprise her. But it is the same man-to-man, no-nonsense attitude beneath which children are quick to detect the affectionate, sympathetic relationship that has made Anne so good at dealing with her younger brothers, for all her protestations that she can only just about last out the holidays in their company!

ELIZABETH AND PHILIP

Now that Charles and Anne are grown up and lead their own lives, Andrew and Edward have stepped into their shoes to provide the Queen and Prince Philip with the youthful companionship they enjoy so much. The boys are a friendly, natural pair, and refreshingly direct. Andrew's brotherly reaction to being told that a writer's current work in 1969 was about Princess Anne, was an incredulous: 'Writing a book about *Anne*? Whatever for?'

Prince Philip has taught all the children to swim, and no doubt Andrew, and then Edward, will receive the same driving instruction their father gave the other two at an early age in the safe and legitimate environment of the Home Park at Windsor. In time they will be off with their father to visit relations in Germany and have their first taste of winter sporting. At Windsor the boys have their train sets in the playroom conveniently next door to Prince Philip's study, and Andrew now goes out with the guns in Scotland and Norfolk and is of an age to learn to shoot. Charles's sojourns at Balmoral are now inevitably much restricted, and Anne usually cuts short her summer holiday in the cause of Eventing, but Andrew and Edward now cajole their father into sailing with them on the lochs around Balmoral.

In the week or so immediately after Christmas the family are all together again at Sandringham, and able to indulge their lusty enjoyment of beach-combing in mid-winter, when they play uproarious and, of necessity, warming games with any findings such as an old tyre, before barbecueing a meal in the shelter of their beach-hut that stands well within sound of the waves.

Finally

BY 1972, the year of her silver wedding anniversary, the Queen will have reigned for twenty years; an infinitesimal time in the history of the earth, only a short span in the history of her own dynasty, but a period condensing much of all the extraordinary things that have happened to the world in the past hundred years.

Yet for all the changes, material, technological, social, moral and environmental, the monarchy remains, not in itself totally unchanged, but stable. Although Gallup polls are not always renowned for reliability, in a number taken over a considerable period the results come up with a remarkable consistency to show that seventy to seventy-five per cent of the people in Britain still consider a monarchy the most satisfactory head of state.

Every country has to have a head of state. Sometimes, as in America, the elected head of state is also head of government, and in the political field this gives one party the unfair benefit of going into battle with all the status and trappings of the presidency behind it, and gives the 'sitting' president a huge advantage. Where a country has both an elected head of state and an elected head of government, the latter is very likely to see that the populace is not distracted from his own activities, by ensuring that the head of state is a fairly colourless, nominal personality.

The Queen, as hereditary head of state, divorced from political partisanship, provides a focus of loyalty that is unaffected by the battle of party politics going on below. By performing, with all the colour and pageantry attached to a transmitted sovereign, added to her own presence and natural talent, most of the time-consuming ceremonial required by every country from its head of state, the Queen is able to free the executive head of government and allow the man in the power position of prime minister to get on with the political executive work which is his job. Another practical contribution of the monarchy is that the Queen, privy to government secrets for about twenty years, and well acquainted with the political figures in this country and with the Commonwealth leaders for the same length of time, is in the unique position of having all the political wisdom of this kind that she has gathered through the years to pass on to those exercising power in this country and elsewhere.

On the less purely practical side, a head of state who is in direct descent from Egbert, the eighth-century, first-acknowledged king of all England, and from William the Conqueror, provides an embodiment of tradition and history, a symbol of stability, that no transitory president, or flag or other figurehead used in non-monarchist countries can possibly provide. And although this may be an irreverent age, it is an undeniable fact that the monarchy is looked up to and admired by a very large proportion of the population.

These more nebulous facets of the advantages of monarchy, if incontestably substantiated, are not easy to define. But it is even more difficult to specify the Queen's exact position as head of the Church. If one of the qualities demanded of someone in this position is to set an example to her people, then the Queen certainly fulfils this demand. By her own regular attendance at worship each Sunday wherever she may happen to be and by her insistence that her children should do the same and, moreover, that they should be confirmed in their faith, she has provided the required example and has brought up her family to be conscientious and practising Christians.

The past twenty-five years have brought the Queen and Prince Philip to a stage in their public life where, as the Duke avers, they may no longer have the glamour of youth or have yet attained the esteem due to age, but which certainly brings none of the 'stuffiness' and the lessening of activity sometimes attributed to middle life. If anything, the Queen is seen more often in public rather than less, and although broadcasting on television does not come easily, she resumed her Christmas message, in its new form, for 1971. During the arduous forty-one hours of actual filming necessary to produce the one-hour and fifty-minute programme of the *Royal Family* film, the Queen co-operated with good humour and a patient willingness to do several times over, in the manner of TV filming, many of the things required of her.

In fact the Queen remains a model of endurance over the frequent photographic sessions that have always been part of her royal life, as willing to ride different horses for an hour on a sultry day in the Home Park at Windsor in the cause of illustrations for a book, as she is adept at coercing her understandably unenthusiastic husband and children into a group for photographs outside Balmoral Castle during their summer holiday.

FINALLY

The Queen and Prince Philip are still indefatigable in making exhaustive and exhausting state visits and Commonwealth tours, and in addition the Duke continues to roam most corners of the world, combining his good work for the royal partnership with opportunities to further his consuming interest in birds and other wild life and their preservation.

It is never easy to keep up with all Prince Philip's occupations. Those concerning young people benefit materially from his belief that basically they are the same as their forebears, and that what has changed is their knowledge and approach and the things that make an impression on them. He thinks it would be very strange if this were not so because their environment is completely different from the one in which their parents grew up.

For years the Duke was one of those crying in the wilderness about the terrifying dangers of world pollution and the necessity, for the very survival of the human race, of conservation and ecological control, and in 1970 these efforts bore fruit in the focusing of world attention on the problem.

He still thinks and writes and speaks about these and innumerable other things, but in addition in 1971 he took on the presidency of the International Equestrian Federation, and with it his usual but somehow slightly surprising interest in its doings, going to meetings, re-drafting its regulations, and no doubt giving the organization a thorough shake-up. He also attended a number of its competitions overseas, including the driving competition in Budapest which he and the Crown Equerry helped to initiate, and where the latter, driving a team lent by the Queen, won the *concours d'élégance*. Now it seems that this new interest in harness horses has led to the Duke's taking up driving as a sport to compensate partially for his giving up polo.

Although Prince Philip says that he is considerably more likely to remove rather than retain obvious passages in his speeches that the press might 'lift', he still suffers at intervals from being quoted out of context. He was disturbed by the rumpus in June 1971 when, just at a delicate stage in the Common Market negotiations, remarks made during his speech to the Royal Agricultural Society of the Commonwealth were quoted and misconstrued as being anti-Common Market in tone. This was unjust to one who had always been very careful not to express any opinion on this particular subject, and whose object on that occasion was to remind his audience of the need to take social as well as economic factors into account when discussing agriculture, whether or not Britain joined the EEC. At some time in recent years a suggestion to the British Columbia Forest Products

Company that the appalling stench emitted by their pulp mill on Vancouver Island might be relieved if someone 'put a sock in it' was also misconstrued.

But such things will happen. The answer to the headline 'Why *did* Philip put his name to this?', which concerned a foreword to a new, glossy, somewhat *Playboy*-type magazine produced by the British Medical Society, is really very simple. The 'dummy' sent to the Duke and to which he was happy to append his name, was later considered unsaleable, and the whole concept re-thought and re-issued without reference to the author of the foreword, which was retained.

To this family the years have brought much happiness. The Queen and Prince Philip have seen their older children grow up into worthwhile people in their own right, quite apart from their status and proven ability in the royal 'trade', and they have seen them both accepted as such at the public level. Now the family pride that used to centre on Charles's effects with trumpet and cello is concerned with those carpentering efforts produced by Andrew in class at school that adorn odd corners in Windsor Castle. Edward is thought capable of developing the most artistic ability of all of them.

Anne, the little girl with whom Prince Philip used to romp, became an adventurous, sometimes argumentive one with a mind tuned to the same wavelength as his – for most of the time. She has grown into a poised, attractive Princess with a sense of humour similar to his, and it was with this elegant daughter that Prince Philip went to Iran in the autumn of 1971 to represent the Queen at the Shah's magnificent celebrations of Persia's long history. The good comradeship of father and daughter is like the special relationship most mothers have with their sons and which the Queen shares with Charles.

The Queen and Prince Philip and their family are very true to themselves, and would be the last people to be persuaded to any form of gimmickry or false publicity. There is a tremendous integrity, and they will never try to present themselves as other than what they are. Certainly neither would lay claim to virtues they do not possess, and they are humanly fallible, and humanly prone to irritation, fatigue, tenseness and most of the idiosyncrasies common to people everywhere. The job they do so well is not easy and would be envied by few, but it is made possible by the complementary partnership they have worked out with the years. The things that the Queen finds difficult to do are some of those that Prince Philip does best, the things about which he gets impatient are those that the Queen takes time and

FINALLY

trouble to work out. Undoubtedly the ease with which her husband makes contact with people has helped the Queen get into touch with people herself. Their personal partnership seems to thrive on periodic absences, but secure in their affection for one another, possibly the Queen recognized right from the start that it would be impossible and exhausting for all concerned for someone of Prince Philip's active, restless temperament to 'stay put' for too long at a time.

On 20 November 1972 the Queen and Prince Philip will be celebrating their silver wedding, and with sincerity and gratitude they will be celebrating the happiness and contentment they have gained together from the years.